THE CORRECT CREED

THAT EVERY MUSLIM MUST BELIEVE

المُعْتَقَدُ الصَّحِيحُ

By the Noble Scholar

ABDUS SALAAM BIN BURJIS

Original First Printing: Shawwaal شَوَّال 1432 – September 2011 Queens, NY

Revised Second Edition: Rajab رَجَب 1446–January 2025

ISBN Number: 9780984660001

Translation: Team Riwayah, Research Division

Formatting and Editing: Abu Nuh Warith Deen Madyun

Acknowledgement: The majority of the translated Quranic verses are from Muhammad Taqi ad-Din al-Hilali and Dr. Muhsin Khan's translation of the Noble Qur'an or Dr. Mustafa Khattab's translation of the Clear Quran.

website. www.rimarket.net **call or text:** 215.668.7637
E. admin@rimarket.net **Twitter:** @RiMarket_/
FB: RiMarket.com/**Instagram:** Riwayah_Publishing

May Allah, The Most High, reward everyone who assisted in this humble effort. We ask Allah by His Beautiful Names and Lofty Attributes to allow this book to be knowledge from which the people benefit until the Day of Judgment.

Printed in the United States of America

فَهْرِس

Table of Contents

بِسْـــــمِ اللَّهِ الرَّحْمَنِ الرَّحِيـــمِ

Translator's Introduction

In the famous narration, reported in Sahih Muslim[1] and in other books of prophetic narrations[2], Umar bin Al-Khattab ﷺ mentions: **"Once we were sitting with the Messenger of Allah ﷺ when a man rose upon us who had very white clothes and very black hair. No sign of travel was seen upon him, nor did anyone from amongst us know him. (He kept coming) until he sat next to the Prophet ﷺ and touched his knees to his knees and put his two hands on his thighs and said, 'Oh Muhammad, inform me about Al-Islam. So, the Messenger of Allah ﷺ said, 'Al-Islam is that you testify that there is no true God except Allah, and none truly deserves to be worshipped except Him alone and that Muhammad is the Messenger of Allah. (It is) to establish the Salat, to pay the Zakat, to fast Ramadan, and to make the pilgrimage to The House (in Mecca) if you can find a way. (The strange man) said, 'You have spoken the truth.' (Umar) said, 'We were amazed that he asked him (the question) and then confirmed (the truthfulness of the answer).' (The stranger) said, 'Then inform me about Al-Iman.' The Prophet ﷺ said, '(It is) that you believe in Allah, The Angels, The Books, The Last Day, and that you believe in The Divine Decree, both the good of it and the bad of it.' (The stranger) said, 'You have spoken the truth.' (The stranger) said, 'Then inform me about Al-Ihsaan.' The Prophet ﷺ said, '(It is) that you worship Allah as if you see Him, and if you do not see Him then He sees you.' (The stranger) said, 'Then inform me about The Hour (i.e. when will the Last Day would occur.)' The Prophet ﷺ said, 'The one being asked is not more knowledgeable about it then the questioner.' (The stranger) said, 'Then inform me about its signs.' The Prophet ﷺ said, 'That the slave woman gives birth to her mistress, and that you see the barefoot naked destitute shepherds**

---

[1] The Book of Faith, Chapter: What is Al-Iman, Al-Islam, Al-Qadr, and the Signs of the Hour.

[2] Collected by Abu Dawud, An-Nasaai, At-Tirmidhi, Al-Imaam Ahmad in his Musnad, and others.

3

competing in constructing high buildings. He (i.e. Umar, the narrator of the hadith) said, 'Then (the stranger) departed. So, I remained for a while, and then The Prophet ﷺ said: 'Oh Umar do you know whom the questioner was?' I said: 'Allah and His Messenger know best.' He said, 'Indeed it was Jibril. He came to teach you your religion.'"

I cited this hadith because it clarifies what the pillars of the Islamic Creed are, the creed of the People of the Prophetic Way. It is to believe in Allah, His Angels, His Messengers ﷺ His Books, The Last Day, and Al-Qadar, with the understanding of the Companions of Allah's Messenger ﷺ. Thus, it is these six things that the Noble Sheikh Abdus Salam bin Burjis began with in his book, following the same order mentioned in the hadith. Also, he explains some of the other important beliefs of Ahl As-Sunnah, such as the correct position concerning the status of the Companions ﷺ and the family of The Messenger of Allah ﷺ, the meaning and the reality of Faith, the correct belief concerning the miracles of righteous people, as well as other important topics related to creed. The Sheikh discusses these topics in a concise manner, such that it is easy for the beginning level student of knowledge and the new Muslim to benefit greatly from this book. I occasionally put some translator's comments or footnotes to facilitate the understanding of what is being translated. With that said, I begin this task seeking the aid of Allah and His blessings by mentioning His Majestic Name.

-Team Riwayah, Research Division

About the Author

We present to you, the reader, a summarized biography of the Sheikh who authored the original Arabic text of this book, such that you can appreciate his status as a scholar of Al-Islam and his qualifications for compiling such a book and thus be comforted about the authenticity of the information therein, Allah willing. This is a short biography about the Sheikh and some of his accomplishments, which we extracted from what one of his students wrote about him, and we found on a website dedicated to the works of the Sheikh. We hope that there is some benefit and enlightenment in it for you about him. May Allah have mercy on the sheikh and pardon us and him and join us together in His Paradise.

Birth & Lineage
His name is Abu Abdur-Rahman Abdus-Salaam bin Burjis ibn Naasir Aal Abdul Kareem. He was born in Riyadh, The Kingdom of Saudi Arabia, in the year 1387 of the Islamic Calendar. Most of that hijri year corresponded with the year 1967 of the Gregorian calendar. He was raised under the care of his father in a household that encouraged religiousness and uprightness. By the time he was thirteen he had finished memorizing the Qur'an and began his quest for Islamic knowledge.

Education and Positions Held
As for his formal studies, the Sheikh attended the College of Islamic Jurisprudence at the University of Imam Muhammad bin Saud in Riyadh, after his primary and secondary education, where he received a bachelor's degree in the year 1410 Hijri. Afterwards, he was appointed as a teacher for a short while at an institute in a town about 106 miles west of Riyadh before he decided to return to advance his formal studies. He then enrolled at a higher learning institute for preparing Islamic judges. There he received a master's degree. Afterwards, he was appointed as a judge at the Ministry of Justice in Saudi Arabia. He asked to be relieved from this position, and resigned from another position which he was given later. Instead, he became a lecturer at The Higher Institute for the Judiciary, the same school he received his master's degree from. In 1422 hijri he received his Doctorate and then was appointed as an

5

assistant professor, which is the academic position he held until his death, may Allah have mercy on him.

In addition to these formal studies, the Sheikh studied with and benefitted from many of the scholars of Saudi Arabia; having attended their lectures, lessons, and their explanations of different classical books. From those he benefitted from was Abdul Aziz bin Baz ﷽, the former Grand Mufti of Saudi Arabia. He also benefitted immensely from Muhammad bin Salih Al-Uthaymin, who he used to travel to Mecca to see as a young man during school breaks to attend his lessons and lectures. He even lived with Sheikh Ibn Al-Uthaymin for a while when the Sheikh's family was not with him. He attended the Sheikh's classes for the explanation of several classical books, and Sheikh Ibn Al-Uthaymin held him in high regard. Abdus-Salaam also studied with several other notable Islamic Scholars. He was known for being a person of very good character and very humble towards his parents, his family, his teachers, and those who would accompany him or sit with him.

His Death

The Sheikh died in a horrifying car accident at a very young age in the year 1425 Hijri which corresponds approximately with the year 2004 according to the Western Calendar. He was only 37 years old according to the Western Calendar. It had been said after his death by several scholars and noblemen that which means in English, "The knowledge of the Sheikh surpassed his age". May Allah have mercy on us and our respected sheikh and brother. May Allah pardon us and him and join us together in Heaven.

Publications

The Sheikh has several books that he authored, from them are those that have been published and printed in Arabic and others which have not yet been printed. Here is just a sampling of some of the books with their Arabic titles and a rough translation of the titles or the subject of the book:

1. القول المبين في حكم الاستهزاء بالمؤمنين
The Clear Statement Concerning the Ruling about Mocking the Believers

2. إيقاف النبيل على حكم التمثيل
A Book about the Ruling on Acting

3. عوائق الطلب
Obstacles a Student of Islamic Knowledge faces in his Quest for Knowledge

4. الإعلام ببعض أحكام السلام

A small book about some of the rulings of giving the greetings of Salaam

5. الاهتمام بالسنن النبوية

The Necessity of Giving Importance to the Prophetic Sunnan

6. المعتقد الصحيح الواجب على كل مسلم اعتقاده

The Correct Creed That Every Muslim Must Believe (i.e., the book translated in front of you now). It was originally a lecture, but then the Sheikh was advised to make it into a book. He published it, and it has undergone many printings and editions.

7. معاملة الحكام في ضوء الكتاب والسنة

A book about the proper way to treat and deal with the Muslim rulers according to the Qur'an and the Sunnah

8. الأحاديثُ النَّبويةُ في ذَمِ العُنصريةِ الجاهليةِ

A collection of Prophetic narrations criticizing racism, ethnocentrism, and tribalism from the times of the pre-Islamic ignorance

Additionally, there are other books which the Sheikh authored in Arabic, which we have not mentioned here, as well as many articles that he wrote and published and many audio recordings of lectures and lessons that he gave that are of great importance and benefit. May Allah make it easy for us to translate some more of them in the future to spread the benefit of the Sheikh's works to the English-speaking audience, ameen!

بِسْمِ اللَّهِ الرَّحْمَنِ الرَّحِيمِ

Author's Introduction[3]

A ll praise belongs to Allah. May the peace and blessings be upon the Messenger of Allah, his family, and all his Companions.

Indeed, the creed of Ahl As-Sunnah wal Jamaa'ah is the true religion which every Muslim must believe. It is the belief of the Messenger of Allah 🕮 and his illustrious Companions—may Allah be pleased with each of them. Whoever opposes them in this doctrine, has subjected himself to Allah's severe punishment, His anger, and His hatred. The (Prophet 🕮) said about the seventy-three groups which will appear within his ummah, **"All of them are in the fire, except one. (That one) is the Jamaa'ah."** This hadith was collected by Imam Ahmad and Abu Dawud from the narrations of Muawiyah 🕮. Ahmad, Ibn Majah, and Ibn Abi Aasim also collected this hadith from the narrations of Anas bin Malik 🕮. The Prophet 🕮 described this group—who are protected from the threat of the fire—saying, **"Whoever are upon what my Companions and I are upon today."** Al-Aajurri collected this hadith in Ash-Shariah (in the narration) reported from Abdullah bin 'Amr 🕮. At-Tabarani also collected it in both (Al-Mu'jam) As-Sagheer and Al-Awsat from the narration of Anas bin Malik 🕮.

This (description) is the hallmark of the People of the Sunnah and Prophetic Tradition—they hold firmly to the path of the Messenger of Allah 🕮 and the way of the Rightly Guided Caliphs, biting down resolutely to (this path) with their molar teeth[4]. Therefore, they are the saved group. They are safe from the fire on Day of Judgment, and they are secure from innovation in

---

[3] The author's introduction was not included in our first printing of this work but has now been added based on the Maktabatu Al-Furqaan printing of *Al-Mu'taqad As-Sahih* (i.e., The Correct Creed), published in Ajman, United Arab Emirates, 2002CE.

[4] **Publisher's Note:** This description truly encapsulates the dire urgency and severity of their adherence.

8

this life. Furthermore, they are the victorious group, based on the Prophet's ﷺ statement regarding them, **"There will never cease to be a (distinct and) dominate group from my Ummah, who will be thaahirun[5] (i.e., victorious) until Allah's affair (i.e., the Day of Judgment) comes."** (This hadith) is collected in Al-Bukhari and Muslim from the narration reported by Al-Mughirah bin Shu'bah ﷺ. The intended meaning of "At-Thuhoor[6]" in this context is victory. Allah said,

$$﴿فَأَيَّدْنَا ٱلَّذِينَ ءَامَنُوا۟ عَلَىٰ عَدُوِّهِمْ فَأَصْبَحُوا۟ ظَٰهِرِينَ ١٤﴾$$

"...So, We gave power to those who believed against their enemies, and they became the victorious (uppermost)." [Saf:14]

And He revealed,

$$﴿ وَإِنَّ جُندَنَا لَهُمُ ٱلْغَٰلِبُونَ ١٧٣ ﴾$$

"And that Our hosts, they verily would be the victors." [As-Saafaat: 173]

So, (Ahl As-Sunnah wal Jamaa'ah) are victorious with the sword and spear (i.e., on the battlefield). And they are triumphant with proofs and evidence. They are one group, not numerous (parties and sects). For this reason, they were named "Al-Jamaa'ah" (i.e., the unified body of Muslims).

Allah said,

$$﴿فَمَاذَا بَعْدَ ٱلْحَقِّ إِلَّا ٱلضَّلَٰلُ﴾$$

"So, after the truth, what else can there be, save error?" [Yunus: 32]

There is no other name by which they are known, other than Islam and Sunnah, or other nicknames that also point to (the meanings of Islam and Sunnah). Imam Malik ﷺ said, **"The people of the Sunnah do not have other names by which they are known, not Jahmi, Qadari, nor Rafidhi."** He was asked about the Sunnah, he responded saying, **"That which has no other name other than 'the Sunnah'."** Meaning, the people of the Sunnah do not ascribe to anything else. The Creed of the pious predecessors (i.e., As-Salaf As-Salih)—which has been explained by many great scholars in various works—is known for its truthfulness and its clear evidence. Sometimes these writings were included in other compilations. While other times they were written as independent books. From amongst these writings are those that were titled

---

[5] ظاهرون

[6] ظهور

9

"As-Sunnah" (i.e., the Creed). There are over 250 publications (with the name "As-Sunnah" or a similar title, which discuss the Correct Islamic Creed). From amongst them:

- As-Sunnah by Ibn Abi Shaybah
- As-Sunnah by Ahmad bin Hanbal
- As-Sunnah by Ibn Abi Aasim
- As-Sunnah by Abdullah bin Ahmad
- As-Sunnah by Al-Khalaal
- As-Sunnah by Ahmad bin Al-Furaat Abi Masood Ar-Raazi
- As-Sunnah by Asad bin Musa
- As-Sunnah by Ibn Al-Qaasim–Imam Malik's colleague
- As-Sunnah by Muhammad bin Salaam Al-Bikandi
- As-Sifaat wa Ar-Radd alaa Al-Jahmiyyah by Nuaym bin Hammaad
- As-Sunnah by Al-Athram
- As-Sunnah by Harb bin Ismaeel Al-Karmaani
- As-Sunnah by Abi Haatim
- As-Sunnah by Ibn Abi Dunyaa
- As-Sunnah and At-Tabseer fee Maalim Ad-Din both by Ibn Jarir At-Tabari
- As-Sunnah by At-Tabaraani
- As-Sunnah by Abu Al-Qaasim Al-Lalakaaee
- As-Sunnah by Muhammad bin Nasr Al-Marwazi

(And other books of creed from the early scholars such as):
- Aqeedatu As-Salaf by As-Saboonee
- Al-Ibanaah by Ibn Battah
- At-Tawheed by Ibn Khuzaymah
- At-Tawheed by Ibn Manda
- Al-Imaan by Ibn Abi Shaybah
- Al-Imaan by Ibn Ubayd Al-Qaasim bin Sallaam
- Sharh As-Sunnah by Al-Muzani-Imam Ash-Shafiee's colleague
- Sharh Madhaahib Ahl As-Sunnah by Ibn Shaaheen
- As-Sunnah (i.e., Al-Hujjah fee Bayaan Al-Mahajjah) by Qiwaam As-Sunnah Abu Al-Qaasim At-Taymee Al-Asbahaani
- Usul As-Sunnah by Abu Abdullah bin Abi Zamaneen
- Ash-Shariah by Al-Aajurri
- Itiqaad Ahl As-Sunnah by Abu Bakr Al-Ismaeeli

- (Sharh) As-Sunnah by Al-Barbahaari
- Al-Imaan by Ibn Manda
- Al-Imaan by Al-Adani
- Al-Arsh by Muhammad bin Abi Shaybah
- Al-Qadr by Ibn Wahb
- Al-Qadr by Abu Dawud
- Ar-Ru'yaa, As-Sifaat, and An-Nuzool all by Ad-Daraqutni
- Risaalatu As-Sijzi ilaa Ahl Az-Zabid by Abu Nasr As-Sijzi
- Jawaab Ahl Damishq fee As-Sifaat by Al-Khateeb Al-Baghdadi
- As-Sunnah by Abu Ahmad As-Asbahaani, known as Al-Assaal
- As-Sunnah by Yaqub Al-Fasawi
- As-Sunnah by Al-Qassaab
- Usul As-Sunnah by Abu Bakr Abdullah bin Az-Zubayr Al-Humaydi
- As-Sunnah by Hanbal bin Ishaaq
- Al-Usul by Abu Amr At-Talamanki

There are countless other books (about the Islamic Creed). Similarly, there are the books of the scholars of Ahl As-Sunnah who came later. These include the writings of Ibn Abdul Barr, Abdul Ghani Al-Maqdisi, Ibn Qudaamah Al-Maqdisi, Ibn Taymiyyah, Ibn Al-Qayyim, Adh-Dhahabi, Ibn Kathir, Muhammad bin Abdul Wahaab, and others. (These books) clarify the correct creed. They contain supporting proofs and evidence, and they expose the doubts of the people of desires.

(In this work, i.e. *The Correct Creed*) we will mention a brief compilation of the beliefs of this (special) elite generation. My success is only with Allah. I rely upon Him alone, and to Him I turn in repentance.

–Abdus Salaam bin Burjis

Section I: The Correct Creed Concerning Allah's Lordship

Ahlus-Sunnah wal Jamaa'ah (i.e. the People of the Prophetic Way and the Group)[7] believe that Allah is alone in His ability to create things, His ownership (of everything), and in His control (over all things). Allah 📿 said,

﴿ إِنَّ رَبَّكُمُ ٱللَّهُ ٱلَّذِى خَلَقَ ٱلسَّمَـٰوَٰتِ وَٱلْأَرْضَ فِى سِتَّةِ أَيَّامٍ ثُمَّ ٱسْتَوَىٰ عَلَى ٱلْعَرْشِ يُغْشِى ٱلَّيْلَ ٱلنَّهَارَ يَطْلُبُهُۥ حَثِيثًا وَٱلشَّمْسَ وَٱلْقَمَرَ وَٱلنُّجُومَ مُسَخَّرَٰتٍ بِأَمْرِهِۦٓ أَلَا لَهُ ٱلْخَلْقُ وَٱلْأَمْرُ تَبَارَكَ ٱللَّهُ رَبُّ ٱلْعَـٰلَمِينَ ۝٥٤ ﴾

"Indeed, your Lord is Allah, Who created the heavens and the earth in Six Days, and then He rose over the Throne. He brings the night as a cover over the day, seeking it rapidly, and (He created) the sun and the moon and the stars subjected to His Command. Surely, His is the Creation and Commandment. Blessed be Allah, the Lord of the 'Aalameen (i.e. mankind, jinn, and all that exists)!" [Al-A'araaf:54]

Allah (📿) said,

﴿ لِّلَّهِ مُلْكُ ٱلسَّمَـٰوَٰتِ وَٱلْأَرْضِ يَخْلُقُ مَا يَشَآءُ يَهَبُ لِمَن يَشَآءُ إِنَـٰثًا وَيَهَبُ لِمَن يَشَآءُ ٱلذُّكُورَ ۝٤٩ ﴾

"To Allah belongs the Kingdom of the Heavens and the Earth. He creates what He wills. He bestows female (offspring) upon whom He wills and

---

[7] **Translator's Note:** Muhammad Salih Al-Uthaymin (may Allah have mercy on him) was asked the question, "Who are Ahlus-Sunnah wal Jamaa'ah?" He replied, "Ahlus-Sunnah wal Jamaa'ah are those who adhere to the Sunnah and unite upon it. They do not turn to (or consider) anything else; not in the knowledge-based matters of belief, nor in the practical issues related to actions. This is why they are called Ahlus- Sunnah (i.e. the People of the Prophetic Way), because they hold fast to it. And they are called Ahlul-Jamaa'ah (i.e. the People of the Group) because they group together upon (the Prophetic Way). If you were to contemplate the state of Ahlul-Bid'ah (i.e. the People of Innovations and Novelties in the religion) you would find them differing in their approaches related to matters of belief and practical matters. This is from those things which indicate that they are far from the Sunnah according to the extent which they have brought innovation (into the religion)." [*Collection of the Religious Verdicts and Letters of Muhammad bin Salih al-Uthaymeen*, Volume 1, Chapter "Ahl As-Sunnah wal Jamaah"]

12

bestows male (offspring) upon whom He wills." [Ash-Shura: 49]

And He (ﷻ) said,

﴿ لَهُۥ مُلۡكُ ٱلسَّمَٰوَٰتِ وَٱلۡأَرۡضِ يُحۡىِۦ وَيُمِيتُۚ وَهُوَ عَلَىٰ كُلِّ شَىۡءٍ قَدِيرٌ ۞ ﴾

"His is the Kingdom of the Heavens and the Earth, it is He Who gives life and causes death; and He is Able to do all things." [Al-Hadeed: 2]

The Idolaters Did Not Dispute Concerning Allah's Oneness in His Lordship

This aspect of Tawhid[8] is called Ar-Ruboobiyyah (i.e. His Lordship over all things, His creating and providing for all things, His giving life and death to all things, and His being All-Powerful over all things). It is that (belief) which is well grounded in the souls of the human being. No one from amongst mankind disputes concerning it whether Muslim or Non-Muslim.[9]

This is as Allah ﷻ said,

﴿ وَلَئِن سَأَلۡتَهُم مَّنۡ خَلَقَ ٱلسَّمَٰوَٰتِ وَٱلۡأَرۡضَ لَيَقُولُنَّ ٱللَّهُۚ قُلِ ٱلۡحَمۡدُ لِلَّهِۚ بَلۡ أَكۡثَرُهُمۡ لَا يَعۡلَمُونَ ۞ ﴾ [لُقۡمَان : ٢٥]

"And if you (Oh Muhammad) ask them, 'Who has created the heavens and the earth?' They will certainly say, 'Allah.' Say, 'Al Hamdu lillah (i.e. all the praises and thanks belong and are due to Allah!)' But most of them know not." [Luqmaan:25]

---

[8] **Translator's Note:** At-Tawhid in the Arabic language literally means to make something one. At-Tawhid in the Islamic terminology is sometimes defined in the following manner: "To single out Allah for all worship," or "to single out Allah in all those things which are exclusively for Him." See Sheikh Ibn Al-Uthaymin's explanation of the book *Kashfush-Shubuhaat* for a similar comprehensive definition.

[9] **Translator's Note:** You may be wondering about the Sheikh's statement that no one from mankind denies this aspect of At-Tawhid and say to yourself, "Rather there are atheists in our times who do not believe in the All-Mighty God, The Creator." The Scholars explained that these people's rejection of the existence of a Creator is only out of obstinacy and arrogance. They outwardly claim to reject the existence of a Creator while deep down they are convinced about His existence. Their rejection is like the rejection of Pharaoh and his followers with regards to The Lord of Moses and the signs from His Lord that he showed them. Allah said concerning Pharaoh and those with him in Surat An-Naml,

﴿ وَجَحَدُواۡ بِهَا وَٱسۡتَيۡقَنَتۡهَآ أَنفُسُهُمۡ ظُلۡمٗا وَعُلُوّٗاۚ فَٱنظُرۡ كَيۡفَ كَانَ عَٰقِبَةُ ٱلۡمُفۡسِدِينَ ۞ ﴾

"And they belied them (i.e. those signs) wrongfully and arrogantly, though their own selves were convinced thereof (i.e. that those signs are from Allah)..." [An-Naml: 14] See *Kitaab At-Tawhid* by Sheikh Saalih Aal-Fawzaan for the like of this explanation.

Allah ﷻ also said concerning (mankind),

$$﴿ وَمَا يُؤْمِنُ أَكْثَرُهُم بِاللَّهِ إِلَّا وَهُم مُّشْرِكُونَ ۝ ﴾$$

"And most of them do not have Iman (i.e. faith) in Allah except that they are Mushrikoon (i.e. ascribe partners to him along with their belief in Him)." [Yusuf: 106]

Mujaahid[10] ﷤ said, "(Most of mankind's) Iman is (merely) their statement: 'Allah (God) is our Creator. He provides for us and causes us to die.' So, this (statement) is (a form of) faith. But it is alongside their associating others with Him in their worship."

The Belief of the Mushrikoon was that their gods are used as a Means of Seeking Nearness to Allah (The All-Mighty God), not that they Create or Provide.

The Mushrikoon (i.e. the pagan Arabs) did not believe that their gods shared with Allah in (His action of) creating. Rather, they believed that this was (the action) of Allah alone, and that their gods were (merely) to be used as a means of seeking nearness to Allah and that they were to be taken as intercessors (on their behalf) to Allah. This is as Allah ﷻ said,

$$﴿ أَلَا لِلَّهِ ٱلدِّينُ ٱلْخَالِصُ وَٱلَّذِينَ ٱتَّخَذُوا۟ مِن دُونِهِۦٓ أَوْلِيَآءَ مَا نَعْبُدُهُمْ إِلَّا لِيُقَرِّبُونَآ إِلَى ٱللَّهِ زُلْفَىٰٓ إِنَّ ٱللَّهَ يَحْكُمُ بَيْنَهُمْ فِى مَا هُمْ فِيهِ يَخْتَلِفُونَ إِنَّ ٱللَّهَ لَا يَهْدِى مَنْ هُوَ كَٰذِبٌ كَفَّارٌ ۝ ﴾$$

"Indeed, sincere devotion is due ˹only˺ to Allah. As for those who take other lords besides Him, ˹saying,˺ "We worship them only so they may bring us closer to Allah," surely Allah will judge between all regarding what they differed about. Allah certainly does not guide whoever persists in lying and disbelief." [Az-Zumar: 3]

And Allah ﷻ said,

$$﴿ قُلْ أَرَءَيْتُمْ شُرَكَآءَكُمُ ٱلَّذِينَ تَدْعُونَ مِن دُونِ ٱللَّهِ أَرُونِى مَاذَا خَلَقُوا۟ مِنَ ٱلْأَرْضِ أَمْ لَهُمْ شِرْكٌ فِى ٱلسَّمَٰوَٰتِ أَمْ ءَاتَيْنَٰهُمْ كِتَٰبًا فَهُمْ عَلَىٰ بَيِّنَتٍ مِّنْهُ بَلْ إِن يَعِدُ ٱلظَّٰلِمُونَ بَعْضُهُم ﴾$$

---

[10] **Translator's Note**: He is Mujaahid Bin Jabr Al-Makkee. He learned explanation of The Qur'an from the companion of The Messenger of Allah ﷺ, Abdullah bin 'Abbaas ﷺ. He is from the foremost of the explainers of The Qur'an from the Muslim nation. The Muslim scholar Adh- Dhahabi said at the end of a biography of Mujaahid, "The Ummah (i.e. Islamic nation) has unanimously agreed about the Imamah (i.e. leadership in his field) of Mujaahid and him (i.e. his statement) being used as evidence."

14

﴿ بَعْضًا إِلَّا غُرُورًا ۝ ﴾

"Say (Oh Muhammad): 'Tell me or inform me (what) do you think about your (so-called) partner-gods whom you call upon besides Allah? Show me, what they have created of the earth. Or have they any share in the heavens?' Or have We given them a Book, so that they act on clear proof from it? No, the wrongdoers promise one another nothing but delusions." [Faatir: 40]

And He ﷻ said concerning the Mushrikoon (i.e. polytheist pagans) of Quraish,

﴿ وَيَقُولُونَ أَئِنَّا لَتَارِكُوٓاْ ءَالِهَتِنَا لِشَاعِرٍ مَّجْنُونٍ ۝ ﴾

"And (they) said: 'Are we going to abandon our gods for the sake of a mad poet?'" [As-Saaffaat: 36]

Allah ﷻ said that they said,

﴿ أَجَعَلَ ٱلْءَالِهَةَ إِلَٰهًا وَٰحِدًا إِنَّ هَٰذَا لَشَىْءٌ عُجَابٌ ۝ ﴾

"Has he reduced ˹all˺ the gods to One God? Indeed, this is something totally astonishing." [Saad: 5]

Verily, Allah confirmed this (aspect of) At-Tawhid to make it firm (in the minds of people), and to use it as proof for the obligation of worshipping Him alone. This is because the oneness of Allah in His Lordship (over all things, His creating and providing for all things, His giving life and death to all things, His being All-Powerful over all things and controlling all things) necessitates that none (deserves) to be worshipped except Allah. And He ﷻ said,

﴿ يَٰٓأَيُّهَا ٱلنَّاسُ ٱعْبُدُواْ رَبَّكُمُ ٱلَّذِى خَلَقَكُمْ وَٱلَّذِينَ مِن قَبْلِكُمْ لَعَلَّكُمْ تَتَّقُونَ ۝ ﴾

"Oh mankind! Worship your Lord, Who created you and those who were before you so that you may have Taqwa (i.e. take precaution from His punishment)." [Al-Baqarah:21]

And He ﷻ said,

﴿ خَلَقَكُم مِّن نَّفْسٍ وَٰحِدَةٍ ثُمَّ جَعَلَ مِنْهَا زَوْجَهَا وَأَنزَلَ لَكُم مِّنَ ٱلْأَنْعَٰمِ ثَمَٰنِيَةَ أَزْوَٰجٍ يَخْلُقُكُمْ فِى بُطُونِ أُمَّهَٰتِكُمْ خَلْقًا مِّنۢ بَعْدِ خَلْقٍ فِى ظُلُمَٰتٍ ثَلَٰثٍ ذَٰلِكُمُ ٱللَّهُ رَبُّكُمْ لَهُ ٱلْمُلْكُ لَآ إِلَٰهَ إِلَّا هُوَ فَأَنَّىٰ تُصْرَفُونَ ۝ ﴾

"He created you (all) from a single soul (i.e. Adam); then made from it its spouse [Hawwa' (Eve)]. And He has sent down for you of cattle eight pairs. He creates you in the wombs of your mothers, creation after creation (i.e. stage after stage) in three veils of darkness; such is Allah your Lord. His is the kingdom, Laa ilaaha illa Huwa (i.e. there is no true God except Him or none deserves to be worshipped except Him). How then are you turned away?" [Az-Zumar: 6]

And He ﷻ said,

﴿ لِإِيلَٰفِ قُرَيْشٍ ۝ إِۦلَٰفِهِمْ رِحْلَةَ ٱلشِّتَآءِ وَٱلصَّيْفِ ۝ فَلْيَعْبُدُواْ رَبَّ هَٰذَا ٱلْبَيْتِ ۝ ٱلَّذِىٓ أَطْعَمَهُم مِّن جُوعٍ وَءَامَنَهُم مِّنْ خَوْفٍ ۝ ﴾

"(At least) for (the favor of) making Quraysh habitually secure—secure in their trading caravan (to Yemen) in the winter and (Syria) in the summer—let them worship the Lord of this (Sacred) House, Who has fed them against hunger and made them secure against fear." [Al-Quraish]

So, Allah ﷻ mentioned that He alone is their Creator and Provider, and this is something they do not doubt concerning. He made that proof upon them for the obligation of devoting (all) worship solely to Him alone, without ascribing partners to Him. He, the Most-High, said,

﴿ قُلِ ٱلْحَمْدُ لِلَّهِ وَسَلَٰمٌ عَلَىٰ عِبَادِهِ ٱلَّذِينَ ٱصْطَفَىٰٓ ءَآللَّهُ خَيْرٌ أَمَّا يُشْرِكُونَ ۝ أَمَّنْ خَلَقَ ٱلسَّمَٰوَٰتِ وَٱلْأَرْضَ وَأَنزَلَ لَكُم مِّنَ ٱلسَّمَآءِ مَآءً فَأَنبَتْنَا بِهِۦ حَدَآئِقَ ذَاتَ بَهْجَةٍ مَّا كَانَ لَكُمْ أَن تُنبِتُواْ شَجَرَهَآ أَءِلَٰهٌ مَّعَ ٱللَّهِ بَلْ هُمْ قَوْمٌ يَعْدِلُونَ ۝ أَمَّن جَعَلَ ٱلْأَرْضَ قَرَارًا وَجَعَلَ خِلَٰلَهَآ أَنْهَٰرًا وَجَعَلَ لَهَا رَوَٰسِىَ وَجَعَلَ بَيْنَ ٱلْبَحْرَيْنِ حَاجِزًا أَءِلَٰهٌ مَّعَ ٱللَّهِ بَلْ أَكْثَرُهُمْ لَا يَعْلَمُونَ ۝ أَمَّن يُجِيبُ ٱلْمُضْطَرَّ إِذَا دَعَاهُ وَيَكْشِفُ ٱلسُّوٓءَ وَيَجْعَلُكُمْ خُلَفَآءَ ٱلْأَرْضِ أَءِلَٰهٌ مَّعَ ٱللَّهِ قَلِيلًا مَّا تَذَكَّرُونَ ۝ أَمَّن يَهْدِيكُمْ فِى ظُلُمَٰتِ ٱلْبَرِّ وَٱلْبَحْرِ وَمَن يُرْسِلُ ٱلرِّيَٰحَ بُشْرًۢا بَيْنَ يَدَىْ رَحْمَتِهِۦٓ أَءِلَٰهٌ مَّعَ ٱللَّهِ تَعَٰلَى ٱللَّهُ عَمَّا يُشْرِكُونَ ۝ ﴾

"Say (Oh Muhammad), Al Hamdu lillah (i.e. all praise and thanks belong and are due to Allah), and peace be upon His servants whom He has chosen (for His Message)! Is Allah better, or (all) that you ascribe as partners (to Him)?' Is not He (better than your gods) Who created the heavens and the earth, and sends down rain for you from the sky, whereby We cause to grow wonderful gardens full of beauty and delight? It is not in your ability to cause the growth of their trees. Is there any god besides Allah? Nay, but they are a people who

16

ascribe equals (to Him)! Is not He (better than your gods) Who has made the earth as a fixed abode, and has placed rivers in its midst, and has placed firm mountains therein, and has set a barrier between the two seas. Is there any god besides Allah? Nay, but most of them do not know. Is not He (better than your gods) Who responds to the distressed one, when he calls Him, and Who removes the evil, and makes you inheritors of the earth, generations after generations. Is there any god besides Allah? Little is that you remember! Is not He (better than your gods) Who guides you in the darkness of the land and the sea, and Who sends the winds as heralds of glad tidings, going before His Mercy (i.e. rain)? Is there any god besides Allah? High Exalted be Allah above all that they associate as partners (to Him)!" [An-Naml: 59-63]

In all these Quranic verses, Allah 🕮 criticizes the polytheists, (specifically those who actually) affirm that He 🕮 alone is the Creator of the Heavens and the Earth and that He alone is the one who causes benefit and harm. This affirmation (of His Lordship) will not benefit them since they have deified something else along with Him which they invoke, as they invoke Allah.

This is the very essence of contradiction, which opposes the legislation and the intellect. The one who is unique in (doing) of all these actions as far as creating, providing, and causing life and death then it is right that He should (also) be singled out for all types of obedience. That is why He 🕮 rebuked them with His statement,

$$ \text{﴿ أَءِلَهٌ مَّعَ ٱللَّهِ ﴾} $$

"Is there any ilaah (i.e. deity who deserves worship) besides Allah?"
He, The Most-High, didn't say, "Is there any *creator* with Allah?" (This is) because they did not dispute concerning that (i.e. that Allah is the only Creator.) And Allah 🕮 clarified the invalidity of shirk in ascribing partners to Him in His Lordship. If that was the case, the Heavens and the Earth would fall into ruin. This also is something grasped intuitively by the intellects. Allah, The Most High, said:

$$ \text{﴿ مَا ٱتَّخَذَ ٱللَّهُ مِن وَلَدٍ وَمَا كَانَ مَعَهُۥ مِنْ إِلَٰهٍ إِذًا لَّذَهَبَ كُلُّ إِلَٰهٍ بِمَا خَلَقَ وَلَعَلَا بَعْضُهُمْ عَلَىٰ بَعْضٍ سُبْحَٰنَ ٱللَّهِ عَمَّا يَصِفُونَ ﴾} $$

"No son (or offspring or children) did Allah beget, nor is there any ilaah (i.e. god) along with Him; (if there had been many gods), behold, each god would have taken away what he had created, and some would have tried to overcome others! Glorified be Allah above all that they attribute to Him!"
[Al- Mu'minoon: 91]

17

Section 2: The Correct Creed Concerning the Tawhid of Allah's Names & Attributes

From the totality of the creed of Ahlus-Sunnah wal- Jamaa'ah is that they attribute to Allah that which He attributed to Himself and that which His Messenger ﷺ attributed to Him, in terms of His Most Beautiful Names and Most Perfect Lofty Attributes. They do not go beyond the Qur'an or the authentic narrations of The Messenger ﷺ. They affirm the wordings of these (names and attributes), and they know what they mean in the Arabic language which the Qur'an was sent in. They leave the (knowledge of the) kayfiyyah (i.e. the reality of how they are or how they occur) to Allah ﷻ. Allah alone knows it and He did not inform anyone from mankind about it. So, they approach this critical subject with established Islamic legislative principles. Whoever adheres to (these precepts) is saved from deviation.

Principle 1: Only Describe Allah with those Attributes which are Mentioned in The Qur'an and the Hadith

The first of these (principles) is to affirm that which Allah attributed to Himself or that which His Messenger ﷺ attributed to Him without adding or subtracting (anything).[11] That is because there is no one more knowledgeable about Allah than Himself, as Allah, the Most High, said,

$$﴿قُلْ ءَأَنتُمْ أَعْلَمُ أَمِ ٱللَّهُ وَمَنْ أَظْلَمُ مِمَّن كَتَمَ شَهَٰدَةً عِندَهُۥ مِنَ ٱللَّهِ وَمَا ٱللَّهُ بِغَٰفِلٍ عَمَّا تَعْمَلُونَ ۞﴾$$

"...Say (Oh Muhammad), 'Do you know better or does Allah?' And who is more unjust than he who conceals the testimony he has from Allah? And Allah is not unaware of what you do." [Al-Baqarah: 140]

---

[11] **Translator's Note:** This means we affirm all those attributes mentioned in The Qur'an and the Sunnah without attributing any additional attributes to Allah that we did not find in these two sources of revelation and without subtracting or negating any attributes that are mentioned in them.

And there is no one more knowledgeable about Allah, after Allah than The Messenger of Allah ﷺ. He ﷺ said,

$$\text{﴿ وَمَا يَنطِقُ عَنِ ٱلْهَوَىٰ ۝ إِنْ هُوَ إِلَّا وَحْيٌ يُوحَىٰ ۝ ﴾}$$

"Nor does he (i.e. Muhammad) speak of (his own) desire. It is only an Inspiration that is inspired." [An-Najm: 3,4][12]

Principle 2: Allah Does Not Resemble the Creation

The second (of these established legislative principles) is the declaration that Allah is transcendent above resembling the creatures in His attributes. He ﷺ said,

$$\text{﴿ لَيْسَ كَمِثْلِهِۦ شَىْءٌ ۖ وَهُوَ ٱلسَّمِيعُ ٱلْبَصِيرُ ﴾}$$

"There is nothing like unto Him and He is The All-Hearing, The All-Seeing." [Ash-Shooraa: 11]

He (ﷺ) said:

$$\text{﴿ وَلَمْ يَكُن لَّهُۥ كُفُوًا أَحَدٌ ۝ ﴾}$$

"And there is nothing co-equal or comparable to Him." [Al-Ikhlaas:4]

Principle 3: No One Comprehends the Kayfiyyah[13] of His Attributes

The third of these (principles) is not attempting to comprehend the kayfiyyah of His attributes (i.e. the true nature of how His attributes are). He ﷺ said,

$$\text{﴿ وَلَا يُحِيطُونَ بِهِۦ عِلْمًا ۝ ﴾}$$

"...and they will never encompass anything of His Knowledge." [Taa Haa: 110]

---

[12] **Translator's Note:** This verse makes the author's point clear. Allah is unseen; no one can claim to know about His Attributes except He Himself or someone He has informed about some of His Names and Attributes. When The Prophet Muhammad ﷺ spoke about the unseen, especially the Names and Attributes of Allah, he did not speak from his own thoughts, philosophies, or his imagination. Rather, it was all revelation that Allah revealed to him.

[13] **Translator's Note:** The word kayfiyyah in Arabic could be translated as the manner, method, modality, nature, or state of something. In other words, how something *actually* is or how it occurs.

And He 🕮 said,

$$ ﴿ هَلۡ تَعۡلَمُ لَهُۥ سَمِيًّا ۝ ﴾ $$

"...Do you know of any who is similar to Him?" [Maryam: 65]

So, from His attributes is that which He 🕮 mentioned textually in His statement,

$$ ﴿ ٱلرَّحۡمَـٰنُ عَلَى ٱلۡعَرۡشِ ٱسۡتَوَىٰ ۝ ﴾ $$

"The Most Merciful, over the Throne He rose." [Taa Haa 5]

(Similar verses are mentioned) in various places in The Quran. So, what is gained from it is the affirmation of Allah's ascension over His Throne, a real ascension. We know its meaning, but we are ignorant of its kayfiyyah (i.e. the true manner or method of this ascension, how it occurs.)

The Meaning of Istiwaa over the Throne

Its meaning is al-'uluww (i.e. highness) and al- irtifaa' (i.e. rising). This is (the meaning) that the Arabic language dictates. Ahlus-Sunnah wal-Jamaa'ah have agreed upon this meaning.

The Lack of Comprehension of the Kayfiyyah of Al-Istiwaa

As for the kayfiyyah (i.e. the manner or method) of this istiwaa (i.e. ascension), no one knows it except Allah alone, without a partner.

Mention of the Attributes of Hearing and Vision

Also, from His (attributes) (are those affirmed) in His 🕮 statement,

$$ ﴿ إِنَّ ٱللَّهَ كَانَ سَمِيعًۢا بَصِيرًا ۝ ﴾ $$

"...Truly, Allah is Ever All-Hearer, All-Seer." [An-Nisaa': 58]

What is gained from this verse and other verses of similar meaning, is the ascription of the attribute of hearing to Allah. As-sama' (i.e. hearing) in the Arabic language is to grasp sounds. We attribute to Allah 🕮 hearing by which He hears all noises, (a unique hearing) which does not resemble (the hearing of) the creatures of Allah. We leave (the knowledge of) the kayfiyyah (i.e. the method or manner) of this (hearing) to Allah 🕮. We do not say (for instance), *"How* does He hear?" We do not (even) delve into that (knowledge) because He 🕮 did not inform us of this. Rather, He kept this knowledge to Himself (Majestic and High is He).

The Meaning of the Attribute of Al-Basr

Likewise (is our understanding of the attribute of) al-basr (i.e. vision). It means to grasp those things that are seen. This is like what has been authentically reported in Sahih Muslim on the authority of Abu Musa Al-Ash'aree ﵁ that The Prophet ﷺ said:

Indeed, Allah does not sleep, and it is not befitting for Him to sleep. He lowers the scale and raises it. The deeds of the night are raised to Him before the deeds of the day, and the deeds of the day (are raised to Him) before the deeds of the night. His veil is light, if He were to remove it than the subuhaat (i.e. light, majesty, and splendor) of His Face would burn all that His vision extends to of His creation.[14]

We affirm actual vision for Allah, by which He grasps all seen things. But we do not know the kayfiyyah (i.e. method or manner) of this vision. Rather, we know that which Allah has taught us in His statement,

$$\text{﴿لَيۡسَ كَمِثۡلِهِۦ شَيۡءٞ وَهُوَ ٱلسَّمِيعُ ٱلۡبَصِيرُ ۝﴾}$$

"There is nothing like unto Him and He is The All-Hearing, The All-Seeing." [Ash-Shuraa: 11]

These are examples of the manner (in which) Ahlus-Sunnah wal-Jamaa'ah (i.e. the people of the Prophetic Way and the Group) deal with the names of Allah ﷻ.

---

[14] **Translator's Note:** This means that the whole of creation would burn if Allah removed that which veiled Him from their sight, since Allah's vision extends to all things. Ash-Sheikh Ibn Al-'Uthaymin mentioned this in his explanation of the narration in Sahih Muslim. In the life of this world, seeing Allah is impossible. But in the Afterlife, Allah will make it possible for whomsoever He wishes. Listen to the explanation of Ash-Sheikh Ibn Al-'Uthaymin or other scholars of the Sunnah for the narrations related to this topic in Sahih Muslim to gain this understanding and further details on the subject of seeing Allah.

Section 3: The Correct Creed Concerning Tawhid of Worship [15]

From the totality of the creed of Ahlus-Sunnah (i.e. the people of the Prophetic Way) is their singling out Allah alone for (all) worship. They do not worship alongside Allah any other deity. Rather, they direct all acts of obedience (i.e. devotion or worship) which Allah commanded, whether it is an obligation or a preferred act, to Allah alone without any partners. They do not prostrate, except to Allah. They do not circumambulate around the Ancient House (i.e. the Ka'bah), except for Allah alone. They do not sacrifice (animals) except for Allah. They do not make vows, except to Allah. They do not take oaths (or swear) except by Allah. They do not make tawakkul (i.e. rely) except on Allah. And they do not make du'aa to (i.e. invoke) except Allah. This is Tawhid Al-Uloohiyyah (i.e. declaring Allah's singularity in deserving to be worshipped). He ﷺ said,

﴾ ۞ وَٱعْبُدُواْ ٱللَّهَ وَلَا تُشْرِكُواْ بِهِۦ شَيْـًٔا ﴿

"And worship Allah and do not make anything as a partner with Him in your worship..." [An-Nisaa':36]

He said,

﴾ ۞ وَقَضَىٰ رَبُّكَ أَلَّا تَعْبُدُواْ إِلَّآ إِيَّاهُ ﴿

"And your Lord has decreed that you worship none but Him." [Al-Israa': 23]
And He said,

﴾ وَمَآ أُمِرُوٓاْ إِلَّا لِيَعْبُدُواْ إِلَٰهًا وَٰحِدًا ﴿

---

[15] **Translator's Note:** Sometimes this category of At-Tawhid is referred to as Tawhid Al-Uloohiyyah or Tawhid Al-'Ibaadah. Both phrases mean to single out Allah alone with all forms of worship.

"And they were not ordered except to worship one God." [At-Tawbah: 31]

And Allah, The Most High, said,

$$﴿ وَمَآ أُمِرُوٓاْ إِلَّا لِيَعْبُدُواْ ٱللَّهَ مُخْلِصِينَ لَهُ ٱلدِّينَ حُنَفَآءَ وَيُقِيمُواْ ٱلصَّلَوٰةَ وَيُؤْتُواْ ٱلزَّكَوٰةَ وَذَٰلِكَ دِينُ ٱلْقَيِّمَةِ ۝ ﴾$$

"And they were not ordered except to worship Allah whilst devoting sincerely to Him their religion (i.e. their worship) and being Hunafaa' (i.e. turning away from all other religions which oppose At-Tawhid) and to establish the Salat and give the Zakat and that is the religion (of the nation) that is upright [see Tafsir Ibn Kathir and Tafsir As-Sa'dee]." [Al-Bayyinah: 5]

And He said,

$$﴿ وَمَا خَلَقْتُ ٱلْجِنَّ وَٱلْإِنسَ إِلَّا لِيَعْبُدُونِ ۝ ﴾$$

"And I have not created the Jinn and mankind except to worship Me." [Adh-Dhaariyaat: 56]

And the meaning of "worship Me" is "to worship Me exclusively, and no one else."

The Opposite of At-Tawhid is Ash-Shirk

The opposite of this (At-Tawhid) is (making) Ash-Shirk with Allah (i.e. to ascribe partners to Allah or to worship anything besides Him). May Allah grant us refuge from it. It is the greatest sin by which Allah is disobeyed. He, the Most High said,

$$﴿ إِنَّ ٱللَّهَ لَا يَغْفِرُ أَن يُشْرَكَ بِهِۦ وَيَغْفِرُ مَا دُونَ ذَٰلِكَ لِمَن يَشَآءُ وَمَن يُشْرِكْ بِٱللَّهِ فَقَدِ ٱفْتَرَىٰٓ إِثْمًا عَظِيمًا ۝ ﴾$$

"Indeed, Allah does not forgive that shirk is made with Him (i.e. that partners are ascribed to Him or that anything other than He is worshipped) but He forgives what is less than that for whomsoever He wills. And whoever does shirk (i.e. ascribes partners to Allah or worships anything other than Allah) then he has fabricated an enormous lie." [An-Nisaa':48]

And He ﷻ said,

$$﴿ إِنَّ ٱللَّهَ لَا يَغْفِرُ أَن يُشْرَكَ بِهِۦ وَيَغْفِرُ مَا دُونَ ذَٰلِكَ لِمَن يَشَآءُ وَمَن يُشْرِكْ بِٱللَّهِ فَقَدْ ضَلَّ ضَلَٰلًۢا بَعِيدًا ۝ ﴾$$

"Indeed, Allah does not forgive that shirk is made with Him (i.e. that partners are ascribed to Him or that anything other than He is worshipped) but He forgives what is less than that for whomsoever He wills. And whoever does shirk (i.e. ascribes partners to Him or worships anything other than Him) then he has strayed far away." [An-Nisaa':116]

And He ﷻ said,

﴿ حُنَفَآءَ لِلَّهِ غَيْرَ مُشْرِكِينَ بِهِۦ وَمَن يُشْرِكْ بِٱللَّهِ فَكَأَنَّمَا خَرَّ مِنَ ٱلسَّمَآءِ فَتَخْطَفُهُ ٱلطَّيْرُ أَوْ تَهْوِي بِهِ ٱلرِّيحُ فِي مَكَانٍ سَحِيقٍ ۝ ﴾

"Hunafaa' Lillah (i.e. worshipping none but Allah), not ascribing partners to Him and whoever ascribes partners to Allah, it is as if he has fallen from the sky, and the birds have snatched him, or the wind has blown him to a far-off place." [Al-Hajj: 31]

And He ﷻ said,

﴿ وَإِذْ قَالَ لُقْمَنُ لِٱبْنِهِۦ وَهُوَ يَعِظُهُۥ يَبُنَىَّ لَا تُشْرِكْ بِٱللَّهِ إِنَّ ٱلشِّرْكَ لَظُلْمٌ عَظِيمٌ ۝ ﴾

"And (mention) when Luqmaan said to his son whilst admonishing him, 'Oh son do not do shirk with Allah (i.e. do not ascribe partners to Allah or worship anything besides Him). Indeed Ash-Shirk (i.e. the ascription of partners to Allah or the worship of anything besides Him) is a great wrongdoing." [Luqmaan: 13]

And He ﷻ clarified that Ash-Shirk nullifies the (good) deeds and is something that takes one out of the religion of Islam. Thus He ﷻ said,

﴿ ذَلِكَ هُدَى ٱللَّهِ يَهْدِي بِهِۦ مَن يَشَآءُ مِنْ عِبَادِهِۦ وَلَوْ أَشْرَكُوا لَحَبِطَ عَنْهُم مَّا كَانُوا يَعْمَلُونَ ۝ ﴾

"And if they committed shirk (i.e. ascribed partners to Allah or worshipped anything besides Him) then that which they did (i.e of good deeds) would have been invalidated." [Al-An'aam: 88]

He ﷻ said,

﴿ وَلَقَدْ أُوحِيَ إِلَيْكَ وَإِلَى ٱلَّذِينَ مِن قَبْلِكَ لَئِنْ أَشْرَكْتَ لَيَحْبَطَنَّ عَمَلُكَ وَلَتَكُونَنَّ مِنَ ٱلْخَسِرِينَ ۝ ﴾

"And it has certainly been revealed to you (oh Muhammad) and to those (Messengers) before you that if you were to commit Ash-Shirk (i.e. ascribe partners to Allah or worship anything besides Him) your deeds would surely

be nullified (i.e. in vain) and you would certainly be from the losers."
[Az-Zumar: 65]

In Sahih Muslim, on the authority of Jaabir Bin 'Abdullah 🙵, it is reported that the Messenger of Allah ﷺ said, **"Whoever meets Allah, while not associating something with Him or worshipping something besides Him, will enter Heaven. And whoever meets Allah whilst** *associating* **something with Him or worshipping something besides Him, will enter the Fire."** In Sahih Al-Bukhari, on the authority of Abdullah bin Mas'ood 🙵, it is reported that the Messenger of Allah ﷺ said, **"Whoever dies whilst being one who calls upon a rival with Allah, will enter the Fire."**

Who is a Mushrik?

Whoever directs any type of worship to other than Allah is a mushrik (i.e. polytheist) and a kaafir (i.e. disbeliever).

Du'aa (Supplication) is not to be Made Except to Allah

Du'aa (i.e. prayer, invocation, supplication) is an act of worship that Allah ordered. Whoever makes du'aa to Allah only then he is a muwahhid (i.e. a true monotheist, one who worships Allah alone). And whoever makes du'aa to other than Allah, then he has ascribed partners to Allah, and has worshipped other than Him. Allah, The Most High, said,

$$﴿ وَلَا تَدْعُ مِن دُونِ ٱللَّهِ مَا لَا يَنفَعُكَ وَلَا يَضُرُّكَ فَإِن فَعَلْتَ فَإِنَّكَ إِذًا مِّنَ ٱلظَّٰلِمِينَ ﴿١٠٦﴾ ﴾$$

"And 'Do not invoke, instead of Allah, what can neither benefit nor harm you—for if you do, then you will certainly be one of the wrongdoers," [Yunus: 106]

Allah, The Most High, said,

$$﴿ وَمَن يَدْعُ مَعَ ٱللَّهِ إِلَٰهًا ءَاخَرَ لَا بُرْهَٰنَ لَهُۥ بِهِۦ فَإِنَّمَا حِسَابُهُۥ عِندَ رَبِّهِۦٓ إِنَّهُۥ لَا يُفْلِحُ ٱلْكَٰفِرُونَ ﴿١١٧﴾ ﴾$$

"Whoever invokes, besides Allah, another god—for which they can have no proof—they will surely find their penalty with their Lord. Indeed, the disbelievers will never succeed." [Al-Mu'minoon: 117]

And He, The Most High, said,

$$﴿ وَأَنَّ ٱلْمَسَٰجِدَ لِلَّهِ فَلَا تَدْعُوا۟ مَعَ ٱللَّهِ أَحَدًا ﴿١٨﴾ وَأَنَّهُۥ لَمَّا قَامَ عَبْدُ ٱللَّهِ يَدْعُوهُ كَادُوا۟$$

$$ \text{يَكُونُونَ عَلَيْهِ لِبَدًا ۝ قُلْ إِنَّمَآ أَدْعُواْ رَبِّى وَلَآ أُشْرِكُ بِهِۦٓ أَحَدًا ۝} $$

"And that the masaajid[16] are for Allah, so do not make du'aa to (i.e. call upon or invoke) along with Allah anyone. And that when the slave of Allah (i.e. Muhammad ﷺ) stood up making du'aa to Him (i.e. invoking Him in prayer) they (i.e. the jinn) just made round him a dense crowd as if sticking one over the other (i.e. in order to listen to his recitation). Say (Oh Muhammad) I only make du'aa (i.e. invocation, supplication) to my Lord, and I associate none as partners with Him." [Al-Jinn: 18-20]

And He, The Most High, said,

$$ \text{لَهُۥ دَعْوَةُ ٱلْحَقِّ وَٱلَّذِينَ يَدْعُونَ مِن دُونِهِۦ لَا يَسْتَجِيبُونَ لَهُم بِشَىْءٍ إِلَّا كَبَٰسِطِ كَفَّيْهِ} $$
$$ \text{إِلَى ٱلْمَآءِ لِيَبْلُغَ فَاهُ وَمَا هُوَ بِبَٰلِغِهِۦ وَمَا دُعَآءُ ٱلْكَٰفِرِينَ إِلَّا فِى ضَلَٰلٍ ۝} $$

"Calling upon Him ˹alone˺ is the truth. But those ˹idols˺ the pagans invoke besides Him ˹can˺ never respond to them in any way. ˹It is˺ just like someone who stretches out their hands to water, ˹asking it˺ to reach their mouths, but it can never do so. The calls of the disbelievers are only in vain." [Ar-Ra'd:14]

And He ﷻ said,

$$ \text{وَٱلَّذِينَ يَدْعُونَ مِن دُونِ ٱللَّهِ لَا يَخْلُقُونَ شَيْئًا وَهُمْ يُخْلَقُونَ ۝ أَمْوَٰتٌ غَيْرُ أَحْيَآءٍ وَمَا} $$
$$ \text{يَشْعُرُونَ أَيَّانَ يُبْعَثُونَ ۝} $$

"Those whom they (i.e. the polytheists) invoke besides Allah have not created anything, but are themselves created. (They are) dead, lifeless, and they know not when they will be raised up." [An-Nahl: 20-21]

And He ﷻ said,

$$ \text{فَلَا تَدْعُ مَعَ ٱللَّهِ إِلَٰهًا ءَاخَرَ فَتَكُونَ مِنَ ٱلْمُعَذَّبِينَ ۝} $$

"So do not invoke another god with Allah, lest you be among those who are punished." [Ash-Shu'araa: 213]

And He ﷻ said,

$$ \text{يُولِجُ ٱلَّيْلَ فِى ٱلنَّهَارِ وَيُولِجُ ٱلنَّهَارَ فِى ٱلَّيْلِ وَسَخَّرَ ٱلشَّمْسَ وَٱلْقَمَرَ كُلٌّ يَجْرِى لِأَجَلٍ} $$

---

[16] **Translator's Note:** The masaajid could mean the places where sujood (i.e. prostration) is performed (i.e. the Masjid(s)) or it could mean the bodily limbs that prostration is made on. See Tafsir Ibn Kathir

مُّسَمًّى ذَٰلِكُمُ ٱللَّهُ رَبُّكُمْ لَهُ ٱلْمُلْكُ وَٱلَّذِينَ تَدْعُونَ مِن دُونِهِۦ مَا يَمْلِكُونَ مِن قِطْمِيرٍ ١٣

إِن تَدْعُوهُمْ لَا يَسْمَعُوا دُعَآءَكُمْ وَلَوْ سَمِعُوا مَا ٱسْتَجَابُوا لَكُمْ وَيَوْمَ ٱلْقِيَٰمَةِ يَكْفُرُونَ

بِشِرْكِكُمْ وَلَا يُنَبِّئُكَ مِثْلُ خَبِيرٍ ١٤ ﴾

"He merges the night into the day, and He merges the day into the night. And He has subjected the Sun and the Moon; each runs its course for a term appointed. Such is Allah your Lord; His is the kingdom. And those, whom you make du'aa to (i.e. invoke or call upon) instead of Him, own not even a qitmeer (i.e. the thin membrane over the date-stone). If you make du'aa to (i.e. invoke or call upon) them, they hear not your call, and if (in case) they were to hear, they could not grant it (i.e. your request) to you. And on the Day of Resurrection, they will disown your worshipping of them. And none can inform you (Oh Muhammad) like Him Who is the All-Knower (of each and everything)." [Faatir: 13-14]

And He ﷻ said,

﴿ وَلَئِن سَأَلْتَهُم مَّنْ خَلَقَ ٱلسَّمَٰوَٰتِ وَٱلْأَرْضَ لَيَقُولُنَّ ٱللَّهُ قُلْ أَفَرَءَيْتُم مَّا تَدْعُونَ مِن دُونِ

ٱللَّهِ إِنْ أَرَادَنِيَ ٱللَّهُ بِضُرٍّ هَلْ هُنَّ كَٰشِفَٰتُ ضُرِّهِۦ أَوْ أَرَادَنِي بِرَحْمَةٍ هَلْ هُنَّ مُمْسِكَٰتُ

رَحْمَتِهِۦ قُلْ حَسْبِيَ ٱللَّهُ عَلَيْهِ يَتَوَكَّلُ ٱلْمُتَوَكِّلُونَ ٣٨ ﴾

"And verily if you ask them (Oh Muhammad), 'Who created the heavens and the Earth?' Surely, they will say: 'Allah.' Say, 'Tell me then, the things that you make du'aa to (i.e. invoke) besides Allah, if Allah intended some harm for me, could they remove His harm, or if He (Allah) intended some mercy for me, could they withhold His Mercy?' Say, 'Sufficient for me is Allah; in Him those who trust (i.e. believers) must put their trust." [Az- Zumar: 38]

And He ﷻ said,

﴿ قُلْ أَرَءَيْتُم مَّا تَدْعُونَ مِن دُونِ ٱللَّهِ أَرُونِي مَاذَا خَلَقُوا مِنَ ٱلْأَرْضِ أَمْ لَهُمْ شِرْكٌ فِى

ٱلسَّمَٰوَٰتِ ٱئْتُونِي بِكِتَٰبٍ مِّن قَبْلِ هَٰذَآ أَوْ أَثَٰرَةٍ مِّنْ عِلْمٍ إِن كُنتُمْ صَٰدِقِينَ ٤ وَمَنْ أَضَلُّ

مِمَّن يَدْعُوا مِن دُونِ ٱللَّهِ مَن لَّا يَسْتَجِيبُ لَهُۥ إِلَىٰ يَوْمِ ٱلْقِيَٰمَةِ وَهُمْ عَن دُعَآئِهِمْ

غَٰفِلُونَ ٥ وَإِذَا حُشِرَ ٱلنَّاسُ كَانُوا لَهُمْ أَعْدَآءً وَكَانُوا بِعِبَادَتِهِمْ كَٰفِرِينَ ٦ ﴾

"Say (Oh Muhammad to these pagans), 'Think about all that you make du'aa to (i.e. invoke) besides Allah. Show me! What have they created of the earth? Or have they a share in (the creation of) the heavens? Bring me a Book (revealed) before this, or some trace of knowledge (i.e. some trace of

knowledge in support of your claims), if you are truthful!' And who is more astray than one who makes du'aa to (i.e. calls upon or invokes) besides Allah, such as will not answer him till the Day of Resurrection, and who are (even) unaware of their du'aa (i.e. calls or invocations) to them? And when mankind are gathered (i.e. on the Day of Resurrection), they (i.e. the false deities) will become enemies for them and will deny their worshipping of them."
[Al- Ahqaaf: 4-6]

It has been confirmed in the Sunan (i.e. collections of Prophetic narrations) on the authority of An-Nu'maan Bin Basheer 🙏 who said, "The Messenger of Allah said, **"Ad-du'aa (i.e. invocation, supplication), it is worship."**

The Dispute Between the Messengers (May Allah Bestow His peace and Commendations Upon Them) and Their People is Over This Type of At-Tawhid

This type of At-Tawhid, Tawhid Al-Uloohiyyah (i.e. to single out Allah for all worship), is that in which the dispute between The Messengers (may the peace and commendations of Allah be upon them) and their people occurred.

The Messengers Were Sent for This Type of At-Tawhid

Tawhid Al-Uloohiyyah is what Messengers were sent to clarify and propagate. It is what scriptures were revealed to confirm, elucidate, and be taken as proof for. As Allah 🕮 said,

$$ ﴿ وَلَقَدْ بَعَثْنَا فِى كُلِّ أُمَّةٍ رَّسُولًا أَنِ ٱعْبُدُواْ ٱللَّهَ وَٱجْتَنِبُواْ ٱلطَّٰغُوتَ ﴾ $$

"And We have sent out into every nation a messenger saying, 'Worship Allah and avoid the taaghoot (i.e. false deities).'" [An-Nahl: 36]

And He 🕮 said,

$$ ﴿ وَمَآ أَرْسَلْنَا مِن قَبْلِكَ مِن رَّسُولٍ إِلَّا نُوحِىٓ إِلَيْهِ أَنَّهُۥ لَآ إِلَٰهَ إِلَّآ أَنَا۠ فَٱعْبُدُونِ ﴾ ٢٥ $$

"And we have not sent down any messenger before you except that We revealed to him (saying) that laa ilaaha illaa anaa (i.e. there is no true god but I or there is nothing that truly deserves to be worshipped but I), so worship Me." [Al-Anbiyaa:25]

And He 🕮 said,

$$ ﴿ يُنَزِّلُ ٱلْمَلَٰٓئِكَةَ بِٱلرُّوحِ مِنْ أَمْرِهِۦ عَلَىٰ مَن يَشَآءُ مِنْ عِبَادِهِۦٓ أَنْ أَنذِرُوٓاْ أَنَّهُۥ لَآ إِلَٰهَ إِلَّآ أَنَا۠ فَٱتَّقُونِ ﴾ ٢ $$

"He sends down the Angels with inspiration of His Command to

28

whomsoever of His slaves He pleases (saying), Warn mankind that laa ilaaha illa anaa (i.e. there is no true god but I or there is nothing that truly deserves to be worshipped but I), so fear Me." [An-Nahl: 2]

And The Messengers (may the peace and commendations of Allah be upon them) began with it in their dawah (i.e., calling) of their people to Allah. For every messenger would say to his people,

﴿ٱعْبُدُواْ ٱللَّهَ مَا لَكُم مِّنْ إِلَٰهٍ غَيْرُهُ﴾

"Worship Allah you have no other ilaah (i.e. god) than Him." [Al-A'raf: 59, 65, 73, and 85]

Nuh, Hud, Shuayb, Saalih, and every messenger proclaimed it. May the peace and commendations of Allah be upon them all. And He ﷻ said:

﴿وَإِبْرَٰهِيمَ إِذْ قَالَ لِقَوْمِهِ ٱعْبُدُواْ ٱللَّهَ وَٱتَّقُوهُ ذَٰلِكُمْ خَيْرٌ لَّكُمْ إِن كُنتُمْ تَعْلَمُونَ ۝ إِنَّمَا تَعْبُدُونَ مِن دُونِ ٱللَّهِ أَوْثَٰنًا وَتَخْلُقُونَ إِفْكًا إِنَّ ٱلَّذِينَ تَعْبُدُونَ مِن دُونِ ٱللَّهِ لَا يَمْلِكُونَ لَكُمْ رِزْقًا فَٱبْتَغُواْ عِندَ ٱللَّهِ ٱلرِّزْقَ وَٱعْبُدُوهُ وَٱشْكُرُواْ لَهُۥ إِلَيْهِ تُرْجَعُونَ ۝﴾

"And Abraham when he said to his people, Worship Allah and fear him, that is better for you if you only knew. Indeed you only worship besides Allah awthaan (i.e. idols or false deities) and you invent an enormous lie. Truly those who you worship besides Allah do not own any provisions for you, so seek sustenance from Allah and worship Him and thank Him. To Him you shall return (for judgment.)" [Al-Ankabut: 16-17]

And Allah ﷻ said about His Prophet Yusuf (i.e. Joseph), peace be upon him, (that he said),

﴿يَٰصَٰحِبَيِ ٱلسِّجْنِ ءَأَرْبَابٌ مُّتَفَرِّقُونَ خَيْرٌ أَمِ ٱللَّهُ ٱلْوَٰحِدُ ٱلْقَهَّارُ ۝ مَا تَعْبُدُونَ مِن دُونِهِ إِلَّا أَسْمَآءً سَمَّيْتُمُوهَآ أَنتُمْ وَءَابَآؤُكُم مَّآ أَنزَلَ ٱللَّهُ بِهَا مِن سُلْطَٰنٍ إِنِ ٱلْحُكْمُ إِلَّا لِلَّهِ أَمَرَ أَلَّا تَعْبُدُواْ إِلَّآ إِيَّاهُ ذَٰلِكَ ٱلدِّينُ ٱلْقَيِّمُ وَلَٰكِنَّ أَكْثَرَ ٱلنَّاسِ لَا يَعْلَمُونَ ۝﴾

"Oh two companions of the prison! Are many different lords (gods) better or Allah, The One, The Irresistible? You do not (truly) worship besides Him anything but names, which you have named you and your fathers, (that) for which Allah has not sent down any authority. The command (or the judgment) is for none but Allah. He has commanded that you worship none but Him, that is the (true) straight religion, but most of mankind do not know." [Yusuf: 39-40]

The Mushrikoon (polytheists) Have No Proof for Their Shirk

The mushrikoon have nothing to support their shirk (i.e. ascription of partners to Allah in worship), not from sound logic nor from that which was conveyed from the Messengers (may the peace and commendations of Allah be upon them). Allah ﷻ said:

﴿ وَسْـَٔلْ مَنْ أَرْسَلْنَا مِن قَبْلِكَ مِن رُّسُلِنَآ أَجَعَلْنَا مِن دُونِ ٱلرَّحْمَٰنِ ءَالِهَةً يُعْبَدُونَ ۝ ﴾

"And ask (oh Muhammad) those who We sent before you of Our Messengers if We had made other than Ar-Rahmaan (i.e. The Most-Merciful) deities to be worshipped." [Az- Zukhruf: 45]

The meaning of this is that there were no messengers that called to the worship of gods alongside Allah. Rather all of them, from the first of them to the last of them, called to the worship of Allah (the One True God) alone without any partner. Allah pointed out a logical proof which invalidates the shirk of the polytheists. He ﷻ said,

﴿ قُلْ أَرَءَيْتُم مَّا تَدْعُونَ مِن دُونِ ٱللَّهِ أَرُونِي مَاذَا خَلَقُوا۟ مِنَ ٱلْأَرْضِ أَمْ لَهُمْ شِرْكٌ فِى ٱلسَّمَٰوَٰتِ ٱئْتُونِى بِكِتَٰبٍ مِّن قَبْلِ هَٰذَآ أَوْ أَثَٰرَةٍ مِّنْ عِلْمٍ إِن كُنتُمْ صَٰدِقِينَ ۝ ﴾

"Say (oh Muhammad): 'Have you not seen that which you worship besides Allah? Show me! What have they created from The Earth? Or do they have a share in (the creation of) the Heavens? Come to me with a Book (revealed) before this or some trace of knowledge (i.e. some trace of knowledge to support your claims) if you are truthful." [Al-Ahqaaf: 4]

This is an undeniable, logical proof for the fact that the worship of anything besides Allah is invalid. (All these false deities) did not create anything, nor did they assist in creating anything. Allah alone is solely the one who did (all) that. So why worship them? Also, Allah rejected that there is any textual proof for the mushrikoon (i.e. polytheists), for what they do of shirk (i.e. ascription of partners to Allah or worship of other than Allah), from the Revealed Scriptures or the Messengers that were sent (may the peace and commendations of Allah be upon them). So, it has become clear (by all this) that there is no proof at all for the polytheists. Thus, they are from those who will dwell in the Fire forever and what a wretched end. From what has preceded, it is known that this type of At-Tawhid (i.e. Tawhid Al-Uloohiyyah, to single out Allah alone for worship) is the foremost of obligations and it is the most important of important things. It is the religion which Allah does not accept other than it from anyone.

Section 4: The Correct Creed Concerning the Six Pillars of Iman

From the totality of the creed of Ahlus-Sunnah wal Jamaa'ah is true belief in Allah, the Angels, Allah's Books, the Messengers (may the peace and commendations of Allah be upon them), the Resurrection after Death, and to have faith in Al-Qadar (i.e. the pre-decree of Allah). Having true belief in Allah is to confirm His Lordship[17], His exclusive right to be worshipped[18] alone without any partners, and to believe in His Beautiful Names and Perfect and Complete Attributes[19]. An explanation of this has proceeded.

Belief in the Angels

Believing in the Angels is to believe in their existence and what was mentioned to us of their names and their tasks. Allah ﷻ said,

﴿ءَامَنَ ٱلرَّسُولُ بِمَآ أُنزِلَ إِلَيْهِ مِن رَّبِّهِۦ وَٱلْمُؤْمِنُونَ كُلٌّ ءَامَنَ بِٱللَّهِ وَمَلَٰٓئِكَتِهِۦ وَكُتُبِهِۦ وَرُسُلِهِۦ﴾

"The Messenger believes in what was sent down to him and so do the believers. All of them believe in Allah and His Angels and His Books and His messengers..." [Al-Baqarah: 285]

And He ﷻ said,

﴿ ۞ لَّيْسَ ٱلْبِرَّ أَن تُوَلُّوا۟ وُجُوهَكُمْ قِبَلَ ٱلْمَشْرِقِ وَٱلْمَغْرِبِ وَلَٰكِنَّ ٱلْبِرَّ مَنْ ءَامَنَ بِٱللَّهِ وَٱلْيَوْمِ ٱلْءَاخِرِ وَٱلْمَلَٰٓئِكَةِ وَٱلْكِتَٰبِ وَٱلنَّبِيِّـۧنَ﴾

---

[17] **Translator's Note:** "Ar-Ruboobiyyah" – Allah's Lordship over all things, His creating and providing for all things, giving life and death to all things, His being All-Powerful and in control over all things, etc.

[18] **Translator's Note:** "Al-Uloohiyyah"

[19] **Translator's Note:** "Al-Asmaa was-Sifaat"

"Righteousness is not that you turn your faces to the east or the west, rather righteousness is (the characteristic of) the one who believes in Allah and The Last Day and the Angels and The Book and the Prophets..." [Al-Baqarah: 177]

(It is reported) in Sahih Muslim from the long narration of 'Umar bin Al-Khattaab in which Jibril 🕊 asked the Prophet Muhammad 🕊 about Al-Iman (i.e. Faith). In response, the Prophet 🕊 said, **"Al-Iman is that you believe in Allah, His Angels, His Books, His Messengers, the Last Day, and Al-Qadar (i.e. the pre-decree), the good of it and the bad of it."**

Description of the Angels

Allah has described them in His Book by His statement,

$$ ﴿ وَلَهُۥ مَن فِى ٱلسَّمَـٰوَٰتِ وَٱلۡأَرۡضِۚ وَمَنۡ عِندَهُۥ لَا يَسۡتَكۡبِرُونَ عَنۡ عِبَادَتِهِۦ وَلَا يَسۡتَحۡسِرُونَ ۝ يُسَبِّحُونَ ٱلَّيۡلَ وَٱلنَّهَارَ لَا يَفۡتُرُونَ ۝ ﴾ $$

"To Him belongs whosoever is in the Heavens and on Earth. And those who are near Him (i.e. the Angels) are not too proud to worship Him, nor are they weary (of His worship). They (i.e. the Angels) glorify His Praises night and day, (and) they never slacken (to do so)." [Surah Al-Anbiyaa': 19 and 20]

Allah, The Most High, also said,

$$ ﴿ وَقَالُواْ ٱتَّخَذَ ٱلرَّحۡمَـٰنُ وَلَدٗاۗ سُبۡحَـٰنَهُۥۚ بَلۡ عِبَادٞ مُّكۡرَمُونَ ۝ لَا يَسۡبِقُونَهُۥ بِٱلۡقَوۡلِ وَهُم بِأَمۡرِهِۦ يَعۡمَلُونَ ۝ ﴾ $$

"...Rather they are (but) honored servants. They do not precede Him (i.e. Allah) in speech and they act (only) according to His command." [Al-Anbiyaa': 26, 27]

And He (🕊) said,

$$ ﴿ إِنَّ ٱلَّذِينَ عِندَ رَبِّكَ لَا يَسۡتَكۡبِرُونَ عَنۡ عِبَادَتِهِۦ وَيُسَبِّحُونَهُۥ وَلَهُۥ يَسۡجُدُونَ ۩ ۝ ﴾ $$

"Indeed, those who are with your Lord (i.e. the Angels) are not too proud to worship Him and they glorify Him and to Him they prostrate." [Al-A'raf: 206][20]

---

[20] **Translator's Note:** This verse is a "verse of prostration", meaning it is legislated for the person reciting it to prostrate after finishing it. From what it is legislated to say whilst in this prostration is (what means in English), "My face is prostrated to the One Who created it and made its hearing and sight by His Ability and Strength.

The Angels Are Servants of Allah

They are servants of Allah and amongst the most tremendous of His creatures. But they do not deserve to be worshipped at all. Allah ﷻ said,

﴿ وَيَوْمَ يَحْشُرُهُمْ جَمِيعًا ثُمَّ يَقُولُ لِلْمَلَـٰئِكَةِ أَهَـٰٓؤُلَآءِ إِيَّاكُمْ كَانُوا۟ يَعْبُدُونَ ۝ قَالُوا۟ سُبْحَـٰنَكَ أَنتَ وَلِيُّنَا مِن دُونِهِم ۖ بَلْ كَانُوا۟ يَعْبُدُونَ ٱلْجِنَّ ۖ أَكْثَرُهُم بِهِم مُّؤْمِنُونَ ۝ ﴾

"And on the day when He will gather them all together (and) then He will say to the Angels, 'Was it you that these ones used to worship?' They will say, 'Glory be to You, You are our Wali (i.e. Lord) to the exclusion of them. Rather they used to worship the Jinn, most of them (i.e. these people) having believed them (i.e. the devils from the Jinn).'" [Saba': 40,41][21]

And He ﷻ said,

﴿ وَلَا يَأْمُرَكُمْ أَن تَتَّخِذُوا۟ ٱلْمَلَـٰئِكَةَ وَٱلنَّبِيِّـۧنَ أَرْبَابًا ۗ أَيَأْمُرُكُم بِٱلْكُفْرِ بَعْدَ إِذْ أَنتُم مُّسْلِمُونَ ۝ ﴾

"Nor is it for him to order you to take the Angels or the Prophets as lords. Would he order you with disbelief after you were Muslims?" [Ali-'Imraan: 80]

In Sahih Muslim (it is narrated) on the authority of 'Aaishah (may Allah be pleased with her) who said, **"The Messenger of Allah ﷺ said, 'The Angels were created from light. The Jinn were created from a flame of smokeless fire, and Adam was created from that which has been described to you.'"** From the description of their physical appearance is that they have wings. Some of them have two wings (i.e. two wings on each side), three wings (i.e. three wings on each side), and four wings (i.e. four wings on each side), etc. Allah ﷻ said,

﴿ ٱلْحَمْدُ لِلَّهِ فَاطِرِ ٱلسَّمَـٰوَٰتِ وَٱلْأَرْضِ جَاعِلِ ٱلْمَلَـٰئِكَةِ رُسُلًا أُو۟لِىٓ أَجْنِحَةٍ مَّثْنَىٰ وَثُلَـٰثَ

Therefore, blessed is Allah the Best Creator."

[21] **Translator's Note:** The Angels will disavow themselves from those who used to worship them. They will say that it was the devils from the Jinn, that these people truly used to worship. This is because when they claimed to worship the Angels, they were worshipping the devils from the Jinn who used to whisper to them to worship other than Allah. They believed what these devils were telling them and complied with and obeyed these devils. See tafseer Ibn Kathir, As-Sa'dee, and Al-Jalaalayn for more details.

وَيَزِيدُ فِى ٱلۡخَلۡقِ مَا يَشَآءُۚ إِنَّ ٱللَّهَ عَلَىٰ كُلِّ شَىۡءٍ قَدِيرٌ ۝

"All Praise is for Allah, the Originator of the Heavens and the Earth, Who made the Angels messengers with wings, two or three or four. He increases in creation what He wills. Surely Allah is Most Capable of everything."
[Faatir:1]

It is narrated in Sahih Al-Bukhari on the authority of Ibn Mas'ood ﷺ that the Prophet ﷺ saw Jibril ﷺ and he had six hundred wings.

Their Ability to Change States

Allah has created the Angels, such that they are able to change into beautiful forms, as Gabriel ﷺ appeared to Maryam (i.e. Mary, the mother of Jesus) in the form of a complete and handsome man. Likewise, they appeared to Ibrahim ﷺ when they stopped over by him as honored guests and when they came to Prophet Lut ﷺ to bring down the punishment upon his people, and so forth.

The Refutation of the Statement of the Polytheists: "The Angels are the daughters of Allah"

Allah refuted the polytheists' statement that the Angels are the daughters of Allah ﷻ. He is far removed from all that the wrongdoers say about Him. (In response to their claim) He said,

وَقَالُوا۟ ٱتَّخَذَ ٱلرَّحۡمَٰنُ وَلَدًاۗ سُبۡحَٰنَهُۥۚ بَلۡ عِبَادٌ مُّكۡرَمُونَ ۝ لَا يَسۡبِقُونَهُۥ بِٱلۡقَوۡلِ وَهُم بِأَمۡرِهِۦ يَعۡمَلُونَ ۝ يَعۡلَمُ مَا بَيۡنَ أَيۡدِيهِمۡ وَمَا خَلۡفَهُمۡ وَلَا يَشۡفَعُونَ إِلَّا لِمَنِ ٱرۡتَضَىٰ وَهُم مِّنۡ خَشۡيَتِهِۦ مُشۡفِقُونَ ۝

"And they say, 'The Most Merciful (Allah) has begotten a son (or children).' Glory to Him! Rather they are (but) honored slaves. They do not precede Him in speech, and they act on His Command. He knows what is before them, and what is behind them, and they cannot intercede except for him with whom He (i.e. Allah) is pleased. And they stand in awe for fear of Him." [Al-Anbiyaa': 26-28]

The Most High said,

فَٱسۡتَفۡتِهِمۡ أَلِرَبِّكَ ٱلۡبَنَاتُ وَلَهُمُ ٱلۡبَنُونَ ۝ أَمۡ خَلَقۡنَا ٱلۡمَلَٰٓئِكَةَ إِنَٰثًا وَهُمۡ شَٰهِدُونَ ۝ أَلَآ إِنَّهُم مِّنۡ إِفۡكِهِمۡ لَيَقُولُونَ ۝ وَلَدَ ٱللَّهُ وَإِنَّهُمۡ لَكَٰذِبُونَ ۝ أَصۡطَفَى ٱلۡبَنَاتِ عَلَى ٱلۡبَنِينَ ۝ مَا لَكُمۡ كَيۡفَ تَحۡكُمُونَ ۝ أَفَلَا تَذَكَّرُونَ ۝ أَمۡ لَكُمۡ سُلۡطَٰنٌ مُّبِينٌ ۝ فَأۡتُوا۟ بِكِتَٰبِكُمۡ

$$\text{إِن كُنتُمْ صَـٰدِقِينَ } ۝$$

"Now ask them (Oh Muhammad), 'Are there (only) daughters for your Lord and sons for them?' Or did We create the Angels females while they were witnesses? Truly, it is of their falsehood that they (i.e. the Quraish pagans) say, 'Allah has begotten (i.e. begotten children - their statement that the Angels are the daughters of Allah).' And, indeed, they are liars! Has He (then) chosen daughters rather than sons? What is the matter with you? How do you decide? Will you not then remember? Or is there for you as plain authority (i.e. a clear proof)? Then bring your Book if you are truthful!" [As-Saffaat: 149-157]

Then He ﷻ also said about the Angels:

$$\text{وَمَا مِنَّآ إِلَّا لَهُۥ مَقَامٌ مَّعْلُومٌ } ۝ \text{ وَإِنَّا لَنَحْنُ ٱلصَّآفُّونَ } ۝ \text{ وَإِنَّا لَنَحْنُ ٱلْمُسَبِّحُونَ } ۝$$

"There is not one of us (angels) but has his known place (or position); and verily we (i.e. the Angels), we stand in rows (for the prayers), and verily we (i.e. the Angels), we are they who glorify (Allah's Praises)." [As-Saaffaat:164-166]

JIBRIL ﷺ

From the Angels is Jibril (Gabriel) ﷺ who is entrusted with (bringing down) the revelation. Allah ﷻ said,

$$\text{قُلْ مَن كَانَ عَدُوًّا لِّجِبْرِيلَ فَإِنَّهُۥ نَزَّلَهُۥ عَلَىٰ قَلْبِكَ بِإِذْنِ ٱللَّهِ}$$

"Say (oh Muhammad) whosoever is an enemy to Jibril (Gabriel) then verily he is the one that brought it (i.e. the Qur'aan) down upon your heart by the permission of your Lord..." [Al- Baqarah: 97]

The Prophet ﷺ saw him in Al-Ubtuh, he had 600 wings, the vastness of his physique having covered the horizon. He also saw him the "Night of Ascension", in Heaven. This is as Allah said,

$$\text{وَلَقَدْ رَءَاهُ نَزْلَةً أُخْرَىٰ } ۝ \text{ عِندَ سِدْرَةِ ٱلْمُنتَهَىٰ } ۝ \text{ عِندَهَا جَنَّةُ ٱلْمَأْوَىٰ } ۝$$

"And he (i.e. Muhammad) certainly saw that ˹angel descend˺ a second time at the Lote Tree of the most extreme limit ˹in the seventh heaven˺— near which is the Garden of ˹Eternal˺ Residence" [An-Najm: 13-15]

And he did not see him in his (true) form except on these two occasions. As for all the other times (that he saw Gabriel), then (Gabriel came) in the form of a man, and mostly in the form (of a man named) Dihya Al-Kalbee. Allah said concerning Jibril .

$$\text{﴿ إِنَّهُۥ لَقَوْلُ رَسُولٍ كَرِيمٍ ۝ ذِى قُوَّةٍ عِندَ ذِى ٱلْعَرْشِ مَكِينٍ ۝ مُّطَاعٍ ثَمَّ أَمِينٍ ۝ وَمَا صَاحِبُكُم بِمَجْنُونٍ ۝ وَلَقَدْ رَءَاهُ بِٱلْأُفُقِ ٱلْمُبِينِ ۝ ﴾}$$

"Verily, this is the Word (this Qur'aan brought by) a most honorable messenger [Jibril (Gabriel), from Allah to the Prophet Muhammad], (he is a) possessor of strength (and a possessor of) high rank with the Lord of the Throne. (He is) obeyed (by the angels), trustworthy there (in the heavens). And (Oh people) your companion (Muhammad) is not a madman. And indeed he saw him (i.e. Gabriel) in the clear horizon (towards the east)." [At-Takweer: 19-23]

MIKAA'IL

And from the Angels is Mikaa'il (i.e. Michael) who is entrusted with the raindrops and directing them to wherever Allah orders him to. Imam Ahmad cited (a narration) on the authority of Anas (who mentioned) that the Prophet said to Jibril (Gabriel), **"Why do I not see Mikaa'il (Michael) smiling ever?"** He responded, **"Mikaa'il (i.e. Michael) has not smiled since the Hell-Fire was created."** Allah said,

$$\text{﴿ مَن كَانَ عَدُوًّا لِّلَّهِ وَمَلَـٰٓئِكَتِهِۦ وَرُسُلِهِۦ وَجِبْرِيلَ وَمِيكَىٰلَ فَإِنَّ ٱللَّهَ عَدُوٌّ لِّلْكَـٰفِرِينَ ۝ ﴾}$$

"Whoever is an enemy of Allah, His Angels, Messengers, Jibril (Gabriel), and Mikaal (i.e. Michael) then indeed Allah is an enemy to the disbelievers." [Al-Baqarah: 98]

ISRAAFEEL

(From the Angels) is Israafeel. He is the one who is entrusted with the Soor (i.e. the Horn). He will blow into it three times by the command of His Lord, The Most High: once with a blow that will strike terror into the hearts of the creatures, second with a blow that will cause everyone to swoon except for whomsoever Allah wills to exempt, and last with a blow that will cause the creatures to arise in order to stand before the Lord of all that exists.

These three aforementioned angels are those who The Messenger of Allah mentioned in his night prayer invocation when he said, **"Oh Allah, Lord of Jibril (Gabriel) and Mikaa'il (Michael) and Israafeel, Originator of The Heavens and The Earth, Knower of the unseen and the visible; You judge between Your slaves concerning that which they used to dispute about. Guide me, by your permission, to that which is correct concerning that which was differed about of the truth. Indeed, You guide whomsoever You will to a** straight path."[22] (It is narrated) in the Sunan of An-Nasaa'i on the authority of 'Aaishah (may Allah be pleased with her) that she said, "The Messenger of Allah ﷺ said, "**Oh Allah, Lord of Jibraa'il (Gabriel) and Mikaa'il (Michael) and Lord of Israafeel, I seek refuge in You from the heat of the Fire and from the punishment of the grave.'**"

THE ANGEL OF DEATH ﷺ

From them is Malakul Mawt (i.e. the Angel of Death). He is the one who is entrusted with taking the souls (at the time of death). Allah, the Most High, said,

﴿ * قُلْ يَتَوَفَّىٰكُم مَّلَكُ ٱلْمَوْتِ ٱلَّذِى وُكِّلَ بِكُمْ ثُمَّ إِلَىٰ رَبِّكُمْ تُرْجَعُونَ ۝ ﴾

"**Say, 'Malakul Mawt (i.e. the Angel of Death), who is set over you, will take your souls, then you shall be brought back to your Lord.'**" [As-Sajdah: 11]

THE GUARDIAN ANGELS

From the Angels are those who are entrusted with guarding mankind in all their circumstances, whether they are at their places of residence, traveling, sleeping, or awake. Allah said,

﴿ سَوَآءٌ مِّنكُم مَّنْ أَسَرَّ ٱلْقَوْلَ وَمَن جَهَرَ بِهِۦ وَمَنْ هُوَ مُسْتَخْفٍ بِٱلَّيْلِ وَسَارِبٌ بِٱلنَّهَارِ ۝ لَهُۥ مُعَقِّبَٰتٌ مِّنۢ بَيْنِ يَدَيْهِ وَمِنْ خَلْفِهِۦ يَحْفَظُونَهُۥ مِنْ أَمْرِ ٱللَّهِ إِنَّ ٱللَّهَ لَا يُغَيِّرُ مَا بِقَوْمٍ حَتَّىٰ يُغَيِّرُوا۟ مَا بِأَنفُسِهِمْ وَإِذَآ أَرَادَ ٱللَّهُ بِقَوْمٍ سُوٓءًا فَلَا مَرَدَّ لَهُۥ وَمَا لَهُم مِّن دُونِهِۦ مِن وَالٍ ۝ ﴾

"**It is the same (to Him) whether any of you conceal his speech or declare it openly, whether he be hidden by night or go forth freely by day. For him (i.e. for each person), there are Mu'aqqibaat (i.e. angels in succession), before and behind him. They guard him by the Command of Allah. Indeed, Allah will not change the condition of a people as long as they do not change what is within their selves. But when Allah wills a people's punishment, there can be no turning back of it, and they will find besides Him no protector.**" [Ar-Ra'd:10-11]

Abdullah bin 'Abbaas ﷺ said with regards to His ﷺ statement "**For him, there are Mu'aqqibaat**": 'They are angels that guard (a person) from in front of him and behind him. Then if his qadar (i.e. whatever is pre-ordained for

---

[22] Collected by Muslim

the person) comes, they depart from him."

THE NOBLE SCRIBES

From them are the Noble Scribes. They are those who write down the deeds of the servants, whether good or bad. He ﷻ said,

$$\text{﴿ وَإِنَّ عَلَيْكُمْ لَحَافِظِينَ ۝ كِرَامًا كَاتِبِينَ ۝ يَعْلَمُونَ مَا تَفْعَلُونَ ۝ ﴾}$$

"And indeed there are watchers over you. (They are) kiraaman kaatibeen (i.e. noble ones who are writing). They know (all) that you do." [Al-Infitaar: 10-12.]

The Great Number of Angels (Peace be Upon Them)

The Prophet Muhammad ﷺ informed, "**Verily Al-Bayt Al-Ma'moor** (i.e. name of a place of worship) **in Heaven; 70,000 angels enter it...**" And (it is reported) in another narration "**(70,000 angels) pray in it each day. They do not return to it; that is the last time they enter it.**"[23]

Whosoever Rejects the Existence of Angels Has Disbelieved

Whosoever rejects the existence of the Angels has disbelieved according to the consensus of the Muslims. Allah ﷻ said,

$$\text{﴿ يَا أَيُّهَا الَّذِينَ آمَنُوا آمِنُوا بِاللَّهِ وَرَسُولِهِ وَالْكِتَابِ الَّذِي نَزَّلَ عَلَى رَسُولِهِ وَالْكِتَابِ الَّذِي أَنزَلَ مِن قَبْلُ وَمَن يَكْفُرْ بِاللَّهِ وَمَلَائِكَتِهِ وَكُتُبِهِ وَرُسُلِهِ وَالْيَوْمِ الْآخِرِ فَقَدْ ضَلَّ ضَلَالًا بَعِيدًا ۝ ﴾}$$

"Oh you who believe! Believe in Allah and His Messenger and the Book (i.e. the Qur'aan) which He has sent down to His Messenger, and the Scripture which He sent down to those before (him), and whosoever disbelieves in Allah and His Angels and His Books and His Messengers and the Last Day, then indeed he has strayed far away." [An-Nisaa':136]

---

[23] Authenticated by Al-Albani in Sahih Al-Jami' with a similar wording.

Section 5: Belief in the Revealed Scriptures

As for having Iman (i.e. faith) in the Revealed Scriptures, then indeed Allah ﷻ revealed a (divine) book with every messenger. Just as He ﷻ said,

﴿ لَقَدْ أَرْسَلْنَا رُسُلَنَا بِٱلْبَيِّنَٰتِ وَأَنزَلْنَا مَعَهُمُ ٱلْكِتَٰبَ وَٱلْمِيزَانَ لِيَقُومَ ٱلنَّاسُ بِٱلْقِسْطِ ﴾

"Indeed, We have sent Our messengers with clear proofs and We revealed with them the Scripture and the Balance (the Scale), so that mankind may maintain justice..." [Al-Hadeed: 25]

He ﷻ said,

﴿ كَانَ ٱلنَّاسُ أُمَّةً وَٰحِدَةً فَبَعَثَ ٱللَّهُ ٱلنَّبِيِّـۧنَ مُبَشِّرِينَ وَمُنذِرِينَ وَأَنزَلَ مَعَهُمُ ٱلْكِتَٰبَ بِٱلْحَقِّ لِيَحْكُمَ بَيْنَ ٱلنَّاسِ فِيمَا ٱخْتَلَفُوا۟ فِيهِ وَمَا ٱخْتَلَفَ فِيهِ إِلَّا ٱلَّذِينَ أُوتُوهُ مِنۢ بَعْدِ مَا جَآءَتْهُمُ ٱلْبَيِّنَٰتُ بَغْيَۢا بَيْنَهُمْ فَهَدَى ٱللَّهُ ٱلَّذِينَ ءَامَنُوا۟ لِمَا ٱخْتَلَفُوا۟ فِيهِ مِنَ ٱلْحَقِّ بِإِذْنِهِۦ وَٱللَّهُ يَهْدِى مَن يَشَآءُ إِلَىٰ صِرَٰطٍ مُّسْتَقِيمٍ ﴾ ۝

"Mankind was one community, then Allah sent Prophets with glad tidings and warnings, and with them He sent the Scripture in truth to judge between people in matters wherein they differed. And only those to whom it (i.e. the Scripture) was given differed concerning it after clear proofs had come to them, because of hatred for each other. Then Allah, by His Leave, guided those who believed to the truth of that wherein they differed. And Allah guides whom He wills to a Straight Path." [Al- Baqarah: 213]

We believe in these Scriptures, and we know they are from Allah. (We do this) in compliance with His ﷻ statement:

﴿ قُولُوٓا۟ ءَامَنَّا بِٱللَّهِ وَمَآ أُنزِلَ إِلَيْنَا وَمَآ أُنزِلَ إِلَىٰٓ إِبْرَٰهِـۧمَ وَإِسْمَٰعِيلَ وَإِسْحَٰقَ وَيَعْقُوبَ وَٱلْأَسْبَاطِ وَمَآ أُوتِىَ مُوسَىٰ وَعِيسَىٰ وَمَآ أُوتِىَ ٱلنَّبِيُّونَ مِن رَّبِّهِمْ لَا نُفَرِّقُ بَيْنَ أَحَدٍ مِّنْهُمْ وَنَحْنُ لَهُۥ مُسْلِمُونَ ﴾ ۝

"Say (Oh Muslims), 'We believe in Allah and that which has been sent down to us and that which has been sent down to Ibrahim (Abraham), Ismaa'eel (Ishmael), Ishaaq (Isaac), Ya'qoob (Jacob), and to Al-Asbaat [the offspring of the twelve sons of Jacob], and that which has been given to Musa (Moses) and 'Iesaa (Jesus), and that which has been given to the Prophets from their Lord. We make no distinction between any of them, and to Him (Allah) we have submitted (in Islam).'" [Al- Baqarah:136]

And (in compliance with) His ﷻ statement,

﴿ يَـٰٓأَيُّهَا ٱلَّذِينَ ءَامَنُوٓاْ ءَامِنُواْ بِٱللَّهِ وَرَسُولِهِۦ وَٱلْكِتَـٰبِ ٱلَّذِى نَزَّلَ عَلَىٰ رَسُولِهِۦ وَٱلْكِتَـٰبِ ٱلَّذِىٓ أَنزَلَ مِن قَبْلُ وَمَن يَكْفُرْ بِٱللَّهِ وَمَلَـٰٓئِكَتِهِۦ وَكُتُبِهِۦ وَرُسُلِهِۦ وَٱلْيَوْمِ ٱلْـَٔاخِرِ فَقَدْ ضَلَّ ضَلَـٰلًۢا بَعِيدًا ﴾

"Oh you who believe! Believe in Allah, and His Messenger, and The Book (The Qur'aan), which He has sent down to His Messenger, and The Scripture, which He sent down to those before (him). And whosoever disbelieves in Allah and His Angels and His Books and His Messengers and The Last Day; then indeed he has strayed far away." [An-Nisaa':136]

Likewise (in compliance with) His ﷻ statement,

﴿ وَقُلْ ءَامَنتُ بِمَآ أَنزَلَ ٱللَّهُ مِن كِتَـٰبٍ ﴾

"...And say (Oh Muhammad), 'I believe in whatsoever Allah sent down of Scripture...'" [Ash-Shuraa: 15]

Allah ﷻ said,

﴿ الٓمٓ ذَٰلِكَ ٱلْكِتَـٰبُ لَا رَيْبَ فِيهِ هُدًى لِّلْمُتَّقِينَ ٱلَّذِينَ يُؤْمِنُونَ بِٱلْغَيْبِ وَيُقِيمُونَ ٱلصَّلَوٰةَ وَمِمَّا رَزَقْنَـٰهُمْ يُنفِقُونَ وَٱلَّذِينَ يُؤْمِنُونَ بِمَآ أُنزِلَ إِلَيْكَ وَمَآ أُنزِلَ مِن قَبْلِكَ وَبِٱلْـَٔاخِرَةِ هُمْ يُوقِنُونَ ﴾

"Alif-Laam-Meem. [These letters are one of the miracles of The Qur'aan and none but Allah knows their meanings]. This is the Book (The Qur'aan), whereof there is no doubt, guidance to those who are Al-Muttaqoon (i.e. the pious, the Allah-fearing). Those who believe in the unseen and perform As-Salat (i.e. the Islamic prayer), and spend out of what we have provided for them. And who believe in that which has been sent down to you and in that which was sent down before you (i.e. the previously revealed scriptures like the Torah and the Gospel, etc.) and they believe with certainty in the Afterlife."

[Al-Baqarah: 1-4]

The Revealed Scriptures are from The Speech of Allah ﷻ

We believe that these scriptures are from the Speech of Allah (mighty and majestic is He) not from the speech of other than Him. We believe that Allah ﷻ actually spoke them as He willed, in the manner He desired. So, (from His Speech) is that which is heard from behind a veil without an intermediary (i.e. without an Angel conveying it to the human messenger), just as Allah spoke directly to Musa without an intermediary. Allah ﷻ said,

$$\{ \text{وَلَمَّا جَاءَ مُوسَىٰ لِمِيقَٰتِنَا وَكَلَّمَهُۥ رَبُّهُۥ} \}$$

"And when Musa (Moses) came at the time and place appointed by Us, and his Lord spoke to him..." [Al-A'araaf:143]

And He said,

$$\{ \text{قَالَ يَٰمُوسَىٰٓ إِنِّى ٱصۡطَفَيۡتُكَ عَلَى ٱلنَّاسِ بِرِسَٰلَٰتِى وَبِكَلَٰمِى} \}$$

"He (Allah) said: 'Oh Musa (Moses) I have chosen you above mankind by My Messages, and by My speaking (to you)..." [Al-A'raf: 144]

And from them (i.e. the types of Speech of Allah) is that which Allah ﷻ causes the angelic messenger to hear and orders him to convey to the human messenger. He ﷻ said,

$$\{ * \text{وَمَا كَانَ لِبَشَرٍ أَن يُكَلِّمَهُ ٱللَّهُ إِلَّا وَحۡيًا أَوۡ مِن وَرَآئِ حِجَابٍ أَوۡ يُرۡسِلَ رَسُولًا فَيُوحِىَ بِإِذۡنِهِۦ مَا يَشَآءُ إِنَّهُۥ عَلِىٌّ حَكِيمٌ ۝} \}$$

"It is not for any human being that Allah should speak to him unless (it be) wahyan (i.e. by inspiration), or from behind a veil, or (that) He sends a messenger to reveal what He wills by His Leave. Verily, He is Most High, Most Wise." [Ash- Shooraa:51]

Believing in The Laws That Are in The Scriptures

Likewise, faith in the Scriptures includes believing in the edicts within them and complying with (the Scriptures). It was obligatory upon the nations, upon whom they were revealed, to rule by them.

The Scriptures Confirm Each Other

(Faith in the Scriptures) is to believe that these books confirm each other; they do not contradict.

Some of The Scriptures Abrogating Others is a Reality

(Likewise, this belief in the scriptures) is to believe that it is true that the later Scriptures abrogate the previous ones, as some of the laws of the Torah were abrogated in the Injil (i.e. Gospel). Allah, The Most High, said about Jesus

﴿ وَمُصَدِّقًا لِّمَا بَيْنَ يَدَىَّ مِنَ ٱلتَّوْرَىٰةِ وَلِأُحِلَّ لَكُم بَعْضَ ٱلَّذِى حُرِّمَ عَلَيْكُمْ ﴾

"And I have come confirming that which was before me of the Torah, and to make lawful to you part of what was forbidden to you..." [Ali-'Imraan: 50]

Just as the Qur'an abrogated (all) that came before it of the Heavenly Scriptures. Allah 🕮 said,

﴿ وَأَنزَلْنَآ إِلَيْكَ ٱلْكِتَٰبَ بِٱلْحَقِّ مُصَدِّقًا لِّمَا بَيْنَ يَدَيْهِ مِنَ ٱلْكِتَٰبِ وَمُهَيْمِنًا عَلَيْهِ ﴾

"And We have sent down to you (Oh Muhammad) the Book (i.e. the Qur'an) in truth, confirming the Scripture that came before it and Muhayminan[24] (i.e. a trustee, witness, or judge) over it (i.e. the old Scriptures)..." [al-Maa'idah: 48]

And He 🕮 said,

﴿ وَمَا هُوَ إِلَّا ذِكْرٌ لِّلْعَٰلَمِينَ ۝ ﴾

"And it (i.e. the Qur'aan) is not but a reminder for Al-'Aalameen (i.e. to all of Mankind and the Jinn)." [Al-Qalam: 52]

Faith in the Scriptures of Allah must be in a general manner where He mentioned (them) in general and in specific where He specified (them by name).

The Names of the Scriptures of Allah

Allah 🕮 mentioned the name of some of His Books. (For example) Allah mentioned the Torah which He sent down to Musa (Moses), the Injil (i.e. the Gospel) which He sent down upon 'Iesaa (Jesus), the Zabur which he sent down upon Dawood (David), and the Qur'aan which was sent down upon Muhammad 🕮. Allah mentioned the Suhuf (i.e. Scriptures) of Ibrahim

---

[24] **Translator's Note:** Ibn Kathir says in his explanation of this verse, "...For indeed the name Al-Muhaymin includes all of these, thus it is an ameen (i.e. trustee), a shaahid (i.e. witness), and a haakim (i.e. judge) over every book that came before it. Allah made this Great Book, which He sent down, the last of the Books, the seal of them, the most comprehensive of them, the greatest of them, and the most complete of them, because He gathered in it the good qualities of that which came before it (of the Heavenly Scriptures) and added to it attributes of perfection which are not in other than it..."

(Abraham) and Musa (Moses), may the peace and commendations of Allah be upon them all. We believe in these (aforementioned) Books in this specific manner. Likewise, Allah mentioned there being many (Revealed) Books in general which He did not specifically name at all. So, we also believe in them in this general way. He ﷻ said,

$$ ﴿ وَقُلْ ءَامَنتُ بِمَآ أَنزَلَ ٱللَّهُ مِن كِتَـٰبٍ ﴾ $$

"...And say (Oh Muhammad), 'I believe in whatsoever Allah sent down of Scripture...'" [Ash-Shooraa: 15]

Al-Qur'an Al-Kareem is the Last of the Revealed Books

Al-Qur'an Al-Kareem, which Allah sent down upon our Prophet ﷺ, is the last of the Heavenly Books. Thus, there is no Book after it. It abrogates all Books that came before it. It is a Book for both Mankind and the Jinn.

Allah ﷻ said,

$$ ﴿ وَمَا هُوَ إِلَّا ذِكْرٌ لِّلْعَـٰلَمِينَ ۝ ﴾ $$

"And it is not but a reminder for all of Al-'Aalameen[25]" [Al-Qalam: 52]

It contains all that mankind needs for their religion and their worldly life. Allah ﷻ said,

$$ ﴿ ٱلْيَوْمَ أَكْمَلْتُ لَكُمْ دِينَكُمْ وَأَتْمَمْتُ عَلَيْكُمْ نِعْمَتِى وَرَضِيتُ لَكُمُ ٱلْإِسْلَـٰمَ دِينًا فَمَنِ ٱضْطُرَّ فِى مَخْمَصَةٍ غَيْرَ مُتَجَانِفٍ لِّإِثْمٍ فَإِنَّ ٱللَّهَ غَفُورٌ رَّحِيمٌ ۝ ﴾ $$

"...This day I have perfected your religion for you and completed my favor upon you and have chosen for you Al-Islam as your religion. But as for him who is forced by severe hunger, with no inclination to sin (such can eat the above-mentioned meats), indeed Allah is Oft-Forgiving, Most Merciful." [Al-Maa'idah: 3]

The Qur'aan is Mu'jiz (i.e. an inimitable miracle)

The Quran is inimitable. No one is able to come with the like of it. Allah ﷻ said,

$$ ﴿ قُل لَّئِنِ ٱجْتَمَعَتِ ٱلْإِنسُ وَٱلْجِنُّ عَلَىٰٓ أَن يَأْتُواْ بِمِثْلِ هَـٰذَا ٱلْقُرْءَانِ لَا يَأْتُونَ بِمِثْلِهِۦ وَلَوْ ﴾ $$

---

[25] **Translator's Note:** The term Al-'Aalameen literally means the Worlds, meaning all the various creatures of Allah whether they are humans, animals, angels, jinn or any of Allah's creatures. Here in this verse the term Al-'Aalameen is referring to the Jinn and Mankind since they are the ones who are held responsible for following this heavenly guidance. See Tafsir Al-Jalaalayn for this understanding.

كَانَ بَعْضُهُمْ لِبَعْضٍ ظَهِيرًا ۝

"Say (Oh Muhammad), 'If Mankind and the Jinn were to gather together to come up with the like of this Qur'aan they would not be able to come with its like, even if they helped one another.'" [Al-Israa: 88]

Allah ﷻ said,

۞ لَّا يَأْتِيهِ ٱلْبَٰطِلُ مِنۢ بَيْنِ يَدَيْهِ وَلَا مِنْ خَلْفِهِۦ ۖ تَنزِيلٌ مِّنْ حَكِيمٍ حَمِيدٍ ۝

"Falsehood cannot come to it from before it or behind it, it is sent down by the All-Wise, Worthy of all praise." [Fussilat: 42]

The Qur'aan is Preserved

The Qur'aan is protected from additions and subtractions (being made to it). Allah ﷻ said,

۞ إِنَّا نَحْنُ نَزَّلْنَا ٱلذِّكْرَ وَإِنَّا لَهُۥ لَحَٰفِظُونَ ۝

"Indeed, We have sent down the Reminder (i.e. the Qur'aan) and indeed We shall certainly protect it." [Al-Hijr: 9]

Section 6: Faith in the Messengers

Faith in the Messengers (may the peace and commendations of Allah be upon them all) is by having firm belief that Allah sent a messenger to every nation, summoning them to worship only Allah without ascribing any partners to Him and to reject all that is worshipped besides Him. It is (to have firm belief) that all of them are truthful, trusted, righteous, rightly guided, honorable, obedient, pious, reliable, and guides who are (themselves) well guided. It is to believe that they all conveyed the Messages of Allah. (It is to have firm belief) that Allah took Ibrahim (i.e. Abraham) as a khalil[26] (i.e. the closest type of friend) and that He (also) took Muhammad (may the peace and commendations of Allah be upon them both) as a khalil (i.e. the closest type of friend).[27] (It is to believe that) Allah spoke directly to Musa and raised Idrees to a high place. (It includes belief) that Jesus is the servant and messenger of Allah, and His word[28] cast into Mary and a (created) spirit[29] from Him (i.e. from that which He created).

---

[26] **Translator's Note:** Proof for this is in verse 125 of Surat An- Nisaa'. Imam As-Sa'dee said in his explanation of the verse: **"Al-khullah is the highest type of love, but verily Allah took Ibrahim as a khalil (i.e. very close friend) because he carried out that which he was ordered to do and performed that which he was tested with. Thus, Allah made him an Imam for mankind, took him as a Khalil, and caused him to be highly praised and (commended) in the Worlds."**

[27] **Translator's Note:** Proof that Allah took Prophet Muhammad ﷺ as a khalil is in his statement which is conveyed in Sahih Muslim: **"If I were to take a khalil from the inhabitants of the earth I would take Ibn Abi Qahaafah (i.e. Abu Bakr) as a khalil but your companion (i.e. The Prophet ﷺ is the khalil of Allah."**

[28] **Translator's Note:** His Word is "Kun!" (i.e. "Be!"), that is how Jesus ﷺ came about. Allah said, "Kun (i.e. "Be!") and it was. The Word itself didn't become Jesus ﷺ rather it was by the Word that he came into existence. See Tasfseer Ibn Kathir or Tafsir As-Sa'dee for verse: 171 in Surat An-Nisaa' for this explanation.

[29] **Translator's Note:** "Wa ruhun minhu" this phrase occurs in verse 171 in Surat An-Nisaa'. It means: "And a spirit from Him". "From Him", in this case, means from what He (Allah) created. It does not mean physically from within Allah, like

It is (to believe) that Allah preferred some (Prophets) over others, raising some of them over others in rank. It includes the belief that Muhammad ﷺ will be the best of the Children of Adam on The Day of Judgment, and there is no boasting in this. It is (to believe) that their calling, from the first of them to the last of them, was the same in terms of the basis of the religion: (the call) to single out Allah in His exclusive right to be worshipped, His Lordship, and His Beautiful Names and Perfect Attributes. Allah, the Most High said,

﴿ إِنَّ ٱلدِّينَ عِندَ ٱللَّهِ ٱلْإِسْلَٰمُ ﴾

"Indeed the only religion with Allah is Al-Islam." [Aal-'Imraan:19][30]

And He said,

﴿ وَمَن يَبْتَغِ غَيْرَ ٱلْإِسْلَٰمِ دِينًا فَلَن يُقْبَلَ مِنْهُ وَهُوَ فِى ٱلْءَاخِرَةِ مِنَ ٱلْخَٰسِرِينَ ۝ ﴾

"And whosoever seeks other than Al-Islam as a religion then it will not be accepted from him, and he in the Afterlife will be from the losers." [Aal-'Imraan: 85]

Allah ﷻ said about Nuh (Noah),

﴿ وَأُمِرْتُ أَنْ أَكُونَ مِنَ ٱلْمُسْلِمِينَ ۝ ﴾

"And I (i.e. Nuh) was ordered to be from amongst the Muslims (i.e. those who submit to Allah's Will)." [Yunus: 72]

And He ﷻ said about Musa (i.e. Moses),

﴿ وَقَالَ مُوسَىٰ يَٰقَوْمِ إِن كُنتُمْ ءَامَنتُم بِٱللَّهِ فَعَلَيْهِ تَوَكَّلُوٓا۟ إِن كُنتُم مُّسْلِمِينَ ۝ ﴾

"And Musa (i.e. Moses) said: 'Oh my people! If you have believed in Allah,

---

Christians say. The usage of "From Him" to mean it is from what He created is also found in verse 13 of Suratul Jaathiyyah:

﴿ وَسَخَّرَ لَكُم مَّا فِى ٱلسَّمَٰوَٰتِ وَمَا فِى ٱلْأَرْضِ جَمِيعًا مِّنْهُ ﴾

"And He has subjected to you all that is in the Heavens and all that is in the Earth; all of it is from Him..." So "from Him" means that He created it, and it is a great blessing and a great favor "from Him". See Tafsir Ibn Kathir for this explanation.

[30] Translator's Note: Here the author quotes several verses indicating all the prophets called to the same creed, though they were sent to different people in different times, and some of the laws that were given to them may have differed. The essence of their message was the same. They all called the people to Al-Islam, the basis of which is to submit oneself in worship to the One and only true God alone without ascribing partners to him.

then put your trust in Him if you are Muslims (i.e. those who submit to Allah's Will)." [Yunus: 84]

And He ﷻ said about Sulaymaan (i.e. Solomon) in the words of Bilqees (i.e. The Queen of Sheba),

﴿قَالَتْ رَبِّ إِنِّى ظَلَمْتُ نَفْسِى وَأَسْلَمْتُ مَعَ سُلَيْمَٰنَ لِلَّهِ رَبِّ ٱلْعَٰلَمِينَ ۝﴾

"'My Lord! Indeed, I have wronged myself and I have made Islam (i.e. submitted) along with Sulaymaan (i.e. Solomon) to the Lord of Al-'Aalameen (i.e. all of the worlds, all of the creatures)." [An-Naml: 44]

And He ﷻ said,

﴿ ۞ شَرَعَ لَكُم مِّنَ ٱلدِّينِ مَا وَصَّىٰ بِهِۦ نُوحًا وَٱلَّذِىٓ أَوْحَيْنَآ إِلَيْكَ وَمَا وَصَّيْنَا بِهِۦٓ إِبْرَٰهِيمَ وَمُوسَىٰ وَعِيسَىٰٓ أَنْ أَقِيمُوا۟ ٱلدِّينَ وَلَا تَتَفَرَّقُوا۟ فِيهِ كَبُرَ عَلَى ٱلْمُشْرِكِينَ مَا تَدْعُوهُمْ إِلَيْهِ ٱللَّهُ يَجْتَبِىٓ إِلَيْهِ مَن يَشَآءُ وَيَهْدِىٓ إِلَيْهِ مَن يُنِيبُ ۝﴾

"He (Allah) has ordained for you the same religion which He ordained for Nooh (i.e. Noah), and that which We have inspired in you (Oh Muhammad), and that which We ordained for Ibrahim (i.e. Abraham), Musa (i.e. Moses) and 'Iesa (i.e. Jesus); (saying) that you should establish (perform) the Religion, and make no divisions in it (i.e. don't split up into different sects). Intolerable for the Mushrikun (i.e. polytheists) is that to which you (Oh Muhammad) call them. Allah chooses for Himself whom He wills, and guides to Himself the one who turns to Him in repentance and in obedience." [Ash-Shuraa: 13]

The Number of Prophets and Messengers (Peace and Commendations be Upon Them All)

The number of Messengers is 315 and the Prophets are 124,000. This is confirmed in the narrations of The Messenger of Allah ﷺ reported from Abu Umamah and Abu Dharr.[31]

The Difference between a Prophet and a Messenger

The difference between a prophet and a messenger is that a prophet is whosoever Allah gives some revelation to and that person informs with what has been revealed to him. So, if that person along with that (i.e. along with being given some revelation) is sent to someone who is in opposition to the Command of Allah to relay to them a message from Allah then they become a messenger. But as for the one who only acts according to the previous legislations and he himself was not sent to anyone to convey to them a

---

[31] See Sahih Ibn Hibban, As-Silsilah As-Sahihah, and As-Sahih Al-Musnad

message from Allah, then he is a prophet not a messenger. Mujaahid (may Allah have mercy on him) said, **"(One who is) only a prophet is the one who is spoken to and (revelation) is revealed to him but he is not sent as a messenger."** Based on this, every messenger is a prophet, but not every prophet is a messenger.[32]

The Names of the Prophets and the Messengers (peace and commendations be upon them all)

Allah ﷻ specified, by name, for us a portion of them, such as Adam, Nuh, Idrees, Hud, Saalih, Ibrahim, Ismaa'eel, Ishaaq, Ya'qoob, Yusuf, Lut, Shu'ayb Yunus, Musa, Haaroon, Ilyaas, Zachariah, Yahyaa, Al-Yasa', Dhul Kifl, Dawood, Sulaymaan, Ayyub, and He mentioned Al-Asbaat (i.e. the offspring of the twelve sons of Jacob) in a general manner, and 'Iesaa (i.e. Jesus) and Muhammad, may the peace and commendations of Allah be upon them all. Allah told us, from their stories and narratives, that which is sufficient and that in which there is a lesson or opportunity for reflection:

$$﴿ وَرُسُلًا قَدْ قَصَصْنَٰهُمْ عَلَيْكَ مِن قَبْلُ وَرُسُلًا لَّمْ نَقْصُصْهُمْ عَلَيْكَ وَكَلَّمَ ٱللَّهُ مُوسَىٰ تَكْلِيمًا ﴾ ۝$$

"And messengers We have told you about before (oh Muhammad) and Messengers We have not told you about, and to Musa (i.e. Moses) Allah spoke directly." [An-Nisaa': 164]

We believe in all of them, specifically (i.e. by their names) where Allah was specific and in a general manner where Allah mentioned them in general.

The Messengers and Prophets are Humans Whom Allah Honored With Prophethood and Messengership

We believe that the Messengers and Prophets (peace and commendations be upon them all) were humans and have no characteristics of lordship. at all. Allah ﷻ said,

$$﴿ قُلْ إِنَّمَآ أَنَا۠ بَشَرٌ مِّثْلُكُمْ يُوحَىٰٓ إِلَيَّ أَنَّمَآ إِلَٰهُكُمْ إِلَٰهٌ وَٰحِدٌ فَمَن كَانَ يَرْجُوا۟ لِقَآءَ رَبِّهِۦ فَلْيَعْمَلْ عَمَلًا صَٰلِحًا وَلَا يُشْرِكْ بِعِبَادَةِ رَبِّهِۦٓ أَحَدًۢا ﴾ ۝$$

"Say (Oh Muhammad), 'I am only a man like you. It has been revealed to me that your Ilaah (i.e. God) is one Ilaah (i.e. God). So whoever hopes for the Meeting with his Lord, let him work righteousness and not associate anything

---

[32] **Editor's Note**: There's lots of difference of opinion on this topic. For further details, see Muhammad Al-Imam's *The Difference between a Prophet and a Messenger*. And Allah knows best.

in worship with his Lord.'" [Al-Kahf: 110]

Allah ﷻ said,

﴿ قَالَتْ لَهُمْ رُسُلُهُمْ إِن نَّحْنُ إِلَّا بَشَرٌ مِّثْلُكُمْ وَلَٰكِنَّ ٱللَّهَ يَمُنُّ عَلَىٰ مَن يَشَاءُ مِنْ عِبَادِهِۦ وَمَا كَانَ لَنَآ أَن نَّأْتِيَكُم بِسُلْطَٰنٍ إِلَّا بِإِذْنِ ٱللَّهِ وَعَلَى ٱللَّهِ فَلْيَتَوَكَّلِ ٱلْمُؤْمِنُونَ ۝ ﴾

"Their Messengers said to them, 'We are no more than human beings like you, but Allah bestows His Grace upon whomever He wills from His slaves. It is not for us to bring you an authority (i.e. a proof) except by the Permission of Allah. And in Allah (alone) let the believers put their trust'" [Ibrahim: 11]

Allah ﷻ said,

﴿ وَمَآ أَرْسَلْنَا قَبْلَكَ مِنَ ٱلْمُرْسَلِينَ إِلَّآ إِنَّهُمْ لَيَأْكُلُونَ ٱلطَّعَامَ وَيَمْشُونَ فِي ٱلْأَسْوَاقِ وَجَعَلْنَا بَعْضَكُمْ لِبَعْضٍ فِتْنَةً أَتَصْبِرُونَ وَكَانَ رَبُّكَ بَصِيرًا ۝ ﴾

"And We never sent before you (oh Muhammad) any of the Messengers except that indeed they ate food and walked in the markets. And We have made some of you as a trial for others: will you have patience? And your Lord is Ever All-Seeing." [Al-Furqaan: 20]

Allah said,

﴿ قُل لَّآ أَقُولُ لَكُمْ عِندِى خَزَآئِنُ ٱللَّهِ وَلَآ أَعْلَمُ ٱلْغَيْبَ وَلَآ أَقُولُ لَكُمْ إِنِّى مَلَكٌ إِنْ أَتَّبِعُ إِلَّا مَا يُوحَىٰ إِلَيَّ قُلْ هَلْ يَسْتَوِى ٱلْأَعْمَىٰ وَٱلْبَصِيرُ أَفَلَا تَتَفَكَّرُونَ ۝ ﴾

"Say (oh Muhammad), 'I am not saying to you that with me are the treasures of Allah, nor (that) I know the unseen; nor am I saying to you that I am an angel. I only follow what is revealed to me by inspiration.' Say, 'Are the blind and the one who sees equal? Will you not then think?'" [Al-An'aam: 50]
And He said,

﴿ قُل لَّآ أَمْلِكُ لِنَفْسِى نَفْعًا وَلَا ضَرًّا إِلَّا مَا شَاءَ ٱللَّهُ وَلَوْ كُنتُ أَعْلَمُ ٱلْغَيْبَ لَٱسْتَكْثَرْتُ مِنَ ٱلْخَيْرِ وَمَا مَسَّنِىَ ٱلسُّوٓءُ إِنْ أَنَا۠ إِلَّا نَذِيرٌ وَبَشِيرٌ لِّقَوْمٍ يُؤْمِنُونَ ۝ ﴾

"Say (oh Muhammad), 'I possess no power of benefit or hurt to myself except as Allah wills. If I had the knowledge of the unseen, I should have secured for myself an Abundance of good, and no evil should have touched me. I am but a warner, and a bringer of glad tidings unto people who believe.'" [Al-A'araaf: 188]

The Messengers and Prophets are Servants of Allah
We believe they are servants, from the servants of Allah, whom Allah honored

with messengership. And in their most dignified situations He described them with (the attribute of) servitude (to Him), and while praising them (He refers to them as His servants and worshippers).

Our Prophet Muhammad ﷺ is The Seal of the Prophets

We believe that Allah sealed the Messages with the Message of Muhammad ﷺ. Thus, Allah sent him to all the Jinn and Mankind. As He ﷻ said,

$$ ﴿ قُلْ يَـٰٓأَيُّهَا ٱلنَّاسُ إِنِّى رَسُولُ ٱللَّهِ إِلَيْكُمْ جَمِيعًا ﴾ $$

"Say (Oh Muhammad), 'Oh mankind indeed I am The Messenger of Allah to you all...'" [Al-A'araaf: 158]

And He ﷻ said,

$$ ﴿ وَمَآ أَرْسَلْنَـٰكَ إِلَّا رَحْمَةً لِّلْعَـٰلَمِينَ ۝ ﴾ $$

"And We have not sent you except as a mercy for Al-'Aalameen (i.e. Mankind, Jinn, and all of the creatures)." [Al- Anbiyaa':107]

And He ﷻ said,

$$ ﴿ وَمَآ أَرْسَلْنَـٰكَ إِلَّا كَآفَّةً لِّلنَّاسِ بَشِيرًا وَنَذِيرًا وَلَـٰكِنَّ أَكْثَرَ ٱلنَّاسِ لَا يَعْلَمُونَ ۝ ﴾ $$

"And We have not sent you (Oh Muhammad) except as a giver of glad tidings and a warner to all mankind, but most of men know not." [Saba': 28]

And Allah ﷻ informed (of the fact) that He took a pledge from the Prophets (peace be upon them) that if they were to reach the time of our Prophet Muhammad ﷺ that they would follow him. In this there is a clear proof that (Muhammad's ﷺ) message is the seal of the messages and that it abrogates every message that came before it.

Allah, the Most High said,

$$ ﴿ وَإِذْ أَخَذَ ٱللَّهُ مِيثَـٰقَ ٱلنَّبِيِّـۧنَ لَمَآ ءَاتَيْتُكُم مِّن كِتَـٰبٍ وَحِكْمَةٍ ثُمَّ جَآءَكُمْ رَسُولٌ مُّصَدِّقٌ لِّمَا مَعَكُمْ لَتُؤْمِنُنَّ بِهِۦ وَلَتَنصُرُنَّهُۥ قَالَ ءَأَقْرَرْتُمْ وَأَخَذْتُمْ عَلَىٰ ذَٰلِكُمْ إِصْرِى قَالُوٓا۟ أَقْرَرْنَا قَالَ فَٱشْهَدُوا۟ وَأَنَا۠ مَعَكُم مِّنَ ٱلشَّـٰهِدِينَ ۝ فَمَن تَوَلَّىٰ بَعْدَ ذَٰلِكَ فَأُو۟لَـٰٓئِكَ هُمُ ٱلْفَـٰسِقُونَ ۝ ﴾ $$

"And when Allah took the Covenant of the Prophets, saying, 'Take whatever I gave you from the Book and Hikmah (i.e. understanding of the Laws of Allah, etc.), and afterwards there will come to you a Messenger confirming what is with you; you must, then, believe in him and help him.' Allah said, 'Do you agree (to it) and will you take up My Covenant (which I conclude with you)?' They said, 'We agree.' He said, 'Then bear witness; and I am with you among the witnesses (for this).' Then whoever turns away after this, they are the Faasiqoon (i.e. rebellious, those who turn away from Allah's Obedience)." [Aal 'Imraan: 81- 82]

The Messengers' Conveyance of Glad Tidings About Our Prophet Muhammad

The Messengers (may the Peace and commendations of Allah be upon them all) conveyed the glad tidings of Muhammad's ﷺ Message. Allah ﷻ said,

﴿ وَإِذْ قَالَ عِيسَى ٱبْنُ مَرْيَمَ يَٰبَنِىٓ إِسْرَٰٓءِيلَ إِنِّى رَسُولُ ٱللَّهِ إِلَيْكُم مُّصَدِّقًا لِّمَا بَيْنَ يَدَىَّ مِنَ ٱلتَّوْرَىٰةِ وَمُبَشِّرًا بِرَسُولٍ يَأْتِى مِنۢ بَعْدِى ٱسْمُهُۥٓ أَحْمَدُ ۖ فَلَمَّا جَآءَهُم بِٱلْبَيِّنَٰتِ قَالُوا۟ هَٰذَا سِحْرٌ مُّبِينٌ ٦ ﴾

"And when 'Iesa (i.e. Jesus), son of Maryam (i.e. Mary), said, 'Oh Children of Israel! I am the Messenger of Allah to you confirming the Torah, which came before me, and giving glad tidings of a Messenger to come after me, whose name shall be Ahmad. But when he (i.e. this Messenger) came to them with clear proofs, they said, 'This is plain magic.'" [As-Saff: 6]

And He ﷻ said,

﴿ ۞ وَٱكْتُبْ لَنَا فِى هَٰذِهِ ٱلدُّنْيَا حَسَنَةً وَفِى ٱلْءَاخِرَةِ إِنَّا هُدْنَآ إِلَيْكَ ۚ قَالَ عَذَابِىٓ أُصِيبُ بِهِۦ مَنْ أَشَآءُ ۖ وَرَحْمَتِى وَسِعَتْ كُلَّ شَىْءٍ ۚ فَسَأَكْتُبُهَا لِلَّذِينَ يَتَّقُونَ وَيُؤْتُونَ ٱلزَّكَوٰةَ وَٱلَّذِينَ هُم بِـَٔايَٰتِنَا يُؤْمِنُونَ ١٥٦ ٱلَّذِينَ يَتَّبِعُونَ ٱلرَّسُولَ ٱلنَّبِىَّ ٱلْأُمِّىَّ ٱلَّذِى يَجِدُونَهُۥ مَكْتُوبًا عِندَهُمْ فِى ٱلتَّوْرَىٰةِ وَٱلْإِنجِيلِ يَأْمُرُهُم بِٱلْمَعْرُوفِ وَيَنْهَىٰهُمْ عَنِ ٱلْمُنكَرِ وَيُحِلُّ لَهُمُ ٱلطَّيِّبَٰتِ وَيُحَرِّمُ عَلَيْهِمُ ٱلْخَبَٰٓئِثَ وَيَضَعُ عَنْهُمْ إِصْرَهُمْ وَٱلْأَغْلَٰلَ ٱلَّتِى كَانَتْ عَلَيْهِمْ ۚ فَٱلَّذِينَ ءَامَنُوا۟ بِهِۦ وَعَزَّرُوهُ وَنَصَرُوهُ وَٱتَّبَعُوا۟ ٱلنُّورَ ٱلَّذِىٓ أُنزِلَ مَعَهُۥٓ ۙ أُو۟لَٰٓئِكَ هُمُ ٱلْمُفْلِحُونَ ١٥٧ ﴾

"And ordain for us good in this world, and in the Hereafter. Certainly, we have turned to You.' He said, '(As to) My Punishment I afflict therewith whom I will and My Mercy embraces all things. That (Mercy) I shall ordain for those who are the Muttaqoon (i.e. the pious, those who fear Allah), and give Zakat; and those who believe in Our Ayaat (i.e. proofs, evidences, verses, lessons, signs and revelations, etc.); Those who follow the Messenger, the Prophet who is umiyy (i.e. can neither read nor write) whom they find written with them in the Torah and the Injil (i.e. Gospel)...'" [Al-A'araf:

156-157]

In Sahih Muslim, Abu Hurairah ﷺ reported that, "The Messenger of Allah ﷺ said, 'By The One in whose Hand Muhammad's soul is in, there is no one from this Ummah[33] (i.e. nation) whether they be Jew or Christian who hears about me and then dies without having believed in me except that he will be from the companions of The Fire."

Whoever Rejects the Message of Muhammad Has Disbelieved

Whoever rejects the message of Muhammad ﷺ then he has disbelieved in all the Messengers, even the Messenger who he claims to believe in and follow. Allah (ﷻ) said,

$$﴿ كَذَّبَتْ قَوْمُ نُوحٍ ٱلْمُرْسَلِينَ ۝ ﴾$$

"The people of Nuh rejected the Messengers."
[Ash-Shu'aaraa: 105]

(Allah) declared them to be rejecters of all the Messengers even though no messenger preceded Nuh.

Whoever Claims Prophethood After Muhammad ﷺ

We believe that there is no prophet after Muhammad ﷺ. Therefore, whoever claims Prophethood after him has disbelieved. Allah ﷻ said,

$$﴿ وَلَـٰكِن رَّسُولَ ٱللَّهِ وَخَاتَمَ ٱلنَّبِيِّـۧنَ ﴾$$

"...But rather he is The Messenger of Allah and The Seal of The Prophets..."
[Al-Ahzaab: 40]

(It is narrated) in Sahih Muslim on the authority of Abu Hurairah ﷺ that the Prophet ﷺ said, "I have been preferred over the (other) Prophets in six (matters). I have been given jawaamiu'l kalim (i.e. short concise rich speech that is filled with a lot of meaning). I have been aided by fright. The spoils of war have been made permissible for me. The Earth has been made a place of prayer and a means of (ritual) purification for me. I was sent to all the creation, and with me all the Prophets were sealed off."

---

[33] **Translator's Note:** The word Ummah sometimes means nation or community in Arabic. The Scholars of Islam clarify that here, in this narration, it is referring to everyone that the Prophet Muhammad ﷺ was sent to, which is everyone on the earth from his time until the Day of Judgment, from every race and in every region. This is called "Ummat Ad-Da'wah" or the nation whom the Message is propagated to.

Whoever Rejects the Message of a single Prophet or Messenger Has Disbelieved

Allah ﷻ said,

﴿ إِنَّ ٱلَّذِينَ يَكْفُرُونَ بِٱللَّهِ وَرُسُلِهِۦ وَيُرِيدُونَ أَن يُفَرِّقُواْ بَيْنَ ٱللَّهِ وَرُسُلِهِۦ وَيَقُولُونَ نُؤْمِنُ بِبَعْضٍ وَنَكْفُرُ بِبَعْضٍ وَيُرِيدُونَ أَن يَتَّخِذُواْ بَيْنَ ذَٰلِكَ سَبِيلًا ۞ أُوْلَٰٓئِكَ هُمُ ٱلْكَٰفِرُونَ حَقًّا وَأَعْتَدْنَا لِلْكَٰفِرِينَ عَذَابًا مُّهِينًا ۞ وَٱلَّذِينَ ءَامَنُواْ بِٱللَّهِ وَرُسُلِهِۦ وَلَمْ يُفَرِّقُواْ بَيْنَ أَحَدٍ مِّنْهُمْ أُوْلَٰٓئِكَ سَوْفَ يُؤْتِيهِمْ أُجُورَهُمْ وَكَانَ ٱللَّهُ غَفُورًا رَّحِيمًا ۞ ﴾

"Verily, those who disbelieve in Allah and His Messengers and wish to make distinction between Allah and His Messengers (i.e. by believing in Allah and disbelieving in His Messengers) saying, 'We believe in some but reject others', and wish to adopt a way in between; they are truly disbelievers. And We have prepared for the disbelievers a humiliating torment. And those who believe in Allah and His Messengers and make no distinction between any of them (i.e. the Messengers), We shall give them their rewards, and Allah is Ever Oft-Forgiving, Most Merciful." [An- Nisaa':150-152]

Section 7: Faith in the Afterlife

From the correct creed is to believe in the Last Day: the Day of Judgment and all the events and horrible ordeals which will occur on that Day. Ahlus-Sunnah are certain of this, as Allah عَزَّوَجَلَّ said,

﴿ وَبِٱلْأَخِرَةِ هُمْ يُوقِنُونَ ﴾

"...And of the Afterlife they are certain." [Al-Baqarah: 4]

And He, the Most High, said,

﴿ ٱللَّهُ لَآ إِلَٰهَ إِلَّا هُوَ لَيَجْمَعَنَّكُمْ إِلَىٰ يَوْمِ ٱلْقِيَٰمَةِ لَا رَيْبَ فِيهِ وَمَنْ أَصْدَقُ مِنَ ٱللَّهِ حَدِيثًا ۝ ﴾

"Allahu laa ilaaha illaa huwa (i.e. Allah, there is no true god or there is none that truly deserves to be worshipped but Him). Certainly, He will gather you (all) together on the Day of Judgment of which there is no doubt. And who is more truthful than Allah in speech." [An-Nisaa':87]

Allah, the Most High, said,

﴿ وَإِنَّ ٱلسَّاعَةَ لَآتِيَةٌ فَٱصْفَحِ ٱلصَّفْحَ ٱلْجَمِيلَ ۝ ﴾

"...The Hour is surely coming, so overlook (Oh Muhammad) their faults with gracious forgiveness..."[34] [Al-Hijr: 85]

Sheikh Ibn Al-'Uthaymin's Comments About Life in The Grave[35]

(Also) connected with belief in the Last Day is having faith in everything which occurs after death, such as the trial of the grave: questioning of the deceased after his burial about his Lord, his religion, and his prophet. As for those who believe, Allah will make them unwavering, with the statement that stands firm. The one who believed will say, **"My Lord is Allah, my Religion is**

---

[34] **Translator's Note:** Please read from the credible books of Tafsir (i.e. Explanation of The Qur'an) in order to correctly understand this Ayah.

[35]**Important Note:** The following section is not from the original author. I added this section from a book by Sheikh Ibn Al-'Uthaymin whose title translates as: Explanation of the Fundamentals of Faith. The author did not speak about the subject of life in the grave, so I added this section from the book of another scholarly author for further benefit.

Al-Islam, and my Prophet is Muhammad ﷺ." While Allah will cause the wrongdoers to falter; the disbeliever will say **"Ahh, Ahh, I don't know."** The hypocrite or the one who had doubts will say, **"I don't know; I heard the people saying something, so I said it."** As for the punishment of the grave, then it is for the wrongdoers; the hypocrites, and the disbelievers.[36] Allah, the Most High, said

$$﴿ وَلَوْ تَرَىٰ إِذِ ٱلظَّٰلِمُونَ فِى غَمَرَٰتِ ٱلْمَوْتِ وَٱلْمَلَٰٓئِكَةُ بَاسِطُوٓا۟ أَيْدِيهِمْ أَخْرِجُوٓا۟ أَنفُسَكُمُ ٱلْيَوْمَ تُجْزَوْنَ عَذَابَ ٱلْهُونِ بِمَا كُنتُمْ تَقُولُونَ عَلَى ٱللَّهِ غَيْرَ ٱلْحَقِّ وَكُنتُمْ عَنْ ءَايَٰتِهِۦ تَسْتَكْبِرُونَ ۝ ﴾$$

"...And if you could only see when the wrongdoers are in the agonies of death, while the angels are stretching forth their hands (saying), 'Deliver your souls! This day you shall be recompensed with the torment of degradation because of what you used to say against Allah other than the truth. And you used to reject His Ayaat (i.e. proofs, evidences, verses, lessons, signs, revelations, etc.) with disdain!" [Al-An'aam: 93]

He, The Most High, said concerning the people of Pharaoh,

$$﴿ ٱلنَّارُ يُعْرَضُونَ عَلَيْهَا غُدُوًّا وَعَشِيًّا وَيَوْمَ تَقُومُ ٱلسَّاعَةُ أَدْخِلُوٓا۟ ءَالَ فِرْعَوْنَ أَشَدَّ ٱلْعَذَابِ ۝ ﴾$$

"The Fire; they are exposed to it, morning, and evening, and on the Day when the Hour will be established (it will be said to the angels): 'Cause Pharaoh's people to enter the severest torment!'" [Ghaafir: 46]

[It is narrated] in Sahih Muslim from the narration of Zayd Ibn Thaabit that the Prophet ﷺ said, "'If it wasn't for the fact that you wouldn't bury each other I would have prayed to Allah to let you hear from the punishment of the grave that which I hear.' (Zayd said) then he turned his face towards [us] saying: 'Seek refuge in Allah from the punishment of The Fire!' They said: 'We seek refuge in Allah from the punishment of The Fire!' He said: 'Seek refuge in Allah from the punishment of the grave!' They said, 'We seek refuge in Allah from the punishment of the grave!' He said: 'Seek refuge in Allah from the fitan (i.e. trials) that which is apparent of them and that which is not apparent!' They said: 'We seek refuge in Allah from fitan (i.e. trials) that

---

[36] **Translator's Note:** Some of the sinful people, who were believers may receive this punishment as well as we know from the Sunnah. May Allah protect us from it!

which is apparent of them and that which is not apparent!' He said: 'Seek refuge in Allah from the trial of The Dajjaal!' They said: 'We seek refuge in Allah from the trial of The Dajjaal!'

As for the bliss of the grave, then it is for the true believers. Allah, The Most High said,

﴿ إِنَّ ٱلَّذِينَ قَالُوا۟ رَبُّنَا ٱللَّهُ ثُمَّ ٱسْتَقَـٰمُوا۟ تَتَنَزَّلُ عَلَيْهِمُ ٱلْمَلَـٰٓئِكَةُ أَلَّا تَخَافُوا۟ وَلَا تَحْزَنُوا۟ وَأَبْشِرُوا۟ بِٱلْجَنَّةِ ٱلَّتِى كُنتُمْ تُوعَدُونَ ﴿٣٠﴾ ﴾

"Surely those who say, "Our Lord is Allah," and then remain steadfast, the angels descend upon them, ⌜saying, ⌝ "Do not fear, nor grieve. Rather, rejoice in the good news of Paradise, which you have been promised. " [Fussilat: 30]

He, the Most High, said,

﴿ فَلَوْلَآ إِذَا بَلَغَتِ ٱلْحُلْقُومَ ﴿٨٣﴾ وَأَنتُمْ حِينَئِذٍ تَنظُرُونَ ﴿٨٤﴾ وَنَحْنُ أَقْرَبُ إِلَيْهِ مِنكُمْ وَلَـٰكِن لَّا تُبْصِرُونَ ﴿٨٥﴾ فَلَوْلَآ إِن كُنتُمْ غَيْرَ مَدِينِينَ ﴿٨٦﴾ تَرْجِعُونَهَآ إِن كُنتُمْ صَـٰدِقِينَ ﴿٨٧﴾ فَأَمَّآ إِن كَانَ مِنَ ٱلْمُقَرَّبِينَ ﴿٨٨﴾ فَرَوْحٌ وَرَيْحَانٌ وَجَنَّتُ نَعِيمٍ ﴿٨٩﴾ ﴾

"Then why do you not (intervene) when it (i.e. the soul of a dying person) reaches the throat? And you at the moment are looking on. But We (i.e. We with Our angels and Our Knowledge)[37] are nearer to him than you, but you see not. Then why don't you, if you are exempt from the reckoning and recompense, bring back the soul (to its body), if you are truthful? Then, if he (i.e. the dying person) is of the Muqarrabun (i.e. those brought near to Allah), (There is for him) rest and provision, and a Garden of Bliss (Heaven)."
[Al-Waaqi'ah: 83-89]

To the end of what Allah said in this surah. And it is narrated on the authority of Al-Baraa' Ibn 'Aazib (ﷺ) that the Prophet (ﷺ) said concerning the situation of the believer when he answers the two angels (that come to him) in his grave, **"A caller will call out from the sky saying, 'My slave has spoken the truth so furnish him from Al-Jennah (i.e. The Garden, Heaven) and clothe him from Al-Jennah and open up for him a door to Al-Jennah.' He (i.e. the Prophet Muhammad, ﷺ) said, "So some of its (i.e. Heaven's) breeze and fragrance will come to him and his grave will be expanded for him to as far as his vision extends."** This is part of a longer narration which Ahmad and

[37] **Translator's Note:** See Tafsir As-Sa'dee for this explanation of closeness in the verse.

Abu Dawood narrated. [38]

The Resurrection

A part of this (faith in The Afterlife) is having faith in Al-Ba'th (i.e. the Resurrection), which is the bringing to life of the dead (for The Day of Judgment). Allah, exalted is He, said,

﴿ وَنُفِخَ فِى ٱلصُّورِ فَصَعِقَ مَن فِى ٱلسَّمَٰوَٰتِ وَمَن فِى ٱلْأَرْضِ إِلَّا مَن شَآءَ ٱللَّهُ ثُمَّ نُفِخَ فِيهِ أُخْرَىٰ فَإِذَا هُمْ قِيَامٌ يَنظُرُونَ ٦٨ ﴾

"And the Trumpet will be blown, and all who are in the heavens and all who are on the earth will swoon away, except whomsoever Allah wills. Then it will blown a second time and behold, they will be standing, looking on (waiting)." [Az-Zumar: 68]

And He, the Most High, said,

﴿ كَمَا بَدَأْنَآ أَوَّلَ خَلْقٍ نُّعِيدُهُ وَعْدًا عَلَيْنَآ إِنَّا كُنَّا فَٰعِلِينَ ١٠٤ ﴾

"...Just as We started the first creation, We shall repeat it, [it is] a promise binding upon Us. Truly, We shall do it." [Al-Anbiyaa: 104]

The Records of Deeds

Faith in the Records of Deeds [is also part of faith in The Afterlife]. They will either be given [to people] in their right hands or from behind their backs in their left hands. Allah, Exalted is He, said,

﴿ فَأَمَّا مَنْ أُوتِىَ كِتَٰبَهُ بِيَمِينِهِ فَيَقُولُ هَآؤُمُ ٱقْرَءُوا۟ كِتَٰبِيَهْ ١٩ إِنِّى ظَنَنتُ أَنِّى مُلَٰقٍ حِسَابِيَهْ ٢٠ فَهُوَ فِى عِيشَةٍ رَّاضِيَةٍ ٢١ فِى جَنَّةٍ عَالِيَةٍ ٢٢ قُطُوفُهَا دَانِيَةٌ ٢٣ كُلُوا۟ وَٱشْرَبُوا۟ هَنِيٓـًٔا بِمَآ أَسْلَفْتُمْ فِى ٱلْأَيَّامِ ٱلْخَالِيَةِ ٢٤ وَأَمَّا مَنْ أُوتِىَ كِتَٰبَهُ بِشِمَالِهِ فَيَقُولُ يَٰلَيْتَنِى لَمْ أُوتَ كِتَٰبِيَهْ ٢٥ وَلَمْ أَدْرِ مَا حِسَابِيَهْ ٢٦ يَٰلَيْتَهَا كَانَتِ ٱلْقَاضِيَةَ ٢٧ مَآ أَغْنَىٰ عَنِّى مَالِيَهْ ٢٨ هَلَكَ عَنِّى سُلْطَٰنِيَهْ ٢٩ خُذُوهُ فَغُلُّوهُ ٣٠ ثُمَّ ٱلْجَحِيمَ صَلُّوهُ ٣١ ثُمَّ فِى سِلْسِلَةٍ ذَرْعُهَا سَبْعُونَ ذِرَاعًا فَٱسْلُكُوهُ ٣٢ إِنَّهُ كَانَ لَا يُؤْمِنُ بِٱللَّهِ ٱلْعَظِيمِ ٣٣ وَلَا يَحُضُّ عَلَىٰ طَعَامِ ٱلْمِسْكِينِ ٣٤ فَلَيْسَ لَهُ ٱلْيَوْمَ هَٰهُنَا حَمِيمٌ ٣٥ وَلَا طَعَامٌ إِلَّا مِنْ غِسْلِينٍ ٣٦ لَّا يَأْكُلُهُ إِلَّا ٱلْخَٰطِـُٔونَ ٣٧ ﴾

"Then as for him who will be given his Record in his right hand, then he will

---

[38] **Translator's Note:** This is the end of what Sheikh Ibn Al- 'Uthaymin said about life in the grave in the Explanation of the Fundamentals of Faith.

57

say, 'Take, read my Record! Surely, I did believe that I would meet my reckoning!' So he will be in a life well pleasing, in a lofty garden, the Qutoof (i.e. fruits that are picked) of which will be low and near at hand (i.e. easy to pick). Eat and drink at ease for that which you have sent on before you in days past! But as for him who will be given his Record in his left hand, then he will say, 'I wish that I had not been given my Record! And that I had never known how my account is. I wish that it were the end (death)! My wealth has not availed me. My power and arguments (to defend myself) have gone from me!' (It will be said): 'Seize him and fetter him, then throw him in the Blazing Fire, then fasten him with a chain the length of which is seventy cubits! Verily, He used to not believe in Allah, the Most Great. And he did not encourage the feeding of Al-Miskeen (i.e. the poor). So, no friend has he here this Day, nor any food except filth from the washing of wounds. None will eat it except the Khaati'oon (i.e. those who were in error, the sinners, disbelievers, polytheists, etc.)." [Al-Haaqqah: 1-37]

The Scales

Faith in the scales [is also part of faith in The Afterlife]. (Scales) will be set up on The Day of Judgment and no soul will be wronged in the least. Allah, the Most High, said,

$$\text{﴿ فَمَن ثَقُلَتْ مَوَٰزِينُهُۥ فَأُوْلَٰٓئِكَ هُمُ ٱلْمُفْلِحُونَ ۝ ﴾}$$

"Then those whose scales (of good deeds) are heavy, these, they are the successful." [Al-Mu'minoon: 102]

The Intercession

Belief in the shafaa'ah (i.e. the intercession), which will occur at that time, is of different types:

THE GREATEST INTERCESSION - This is specific to the Prophet Muhammad ﷺ It is when the people will ask him to plead [to Allah] on their behalf that (Allah) judges between them.

THE INTERCESSION FOR THE GATES OF HEAVEN TO BE OPENED FOR ITS PEOPLE Likewise, this is something specifically for The Prophet [Muhammad] ﷺ.

THE INTERCESSION TO LIGHTEN THE PUNISHMENT UPON THOSE WHO DESERVE IT- This is also something specific for the Prophet ﷺ to do. He will plead on behalf of his uncle, Abu Talib, that the punishment upon him in the hellfire be lightened. This a compensation for the fact that Abu Talib used to protect

Prophet Muhammad ﷺ and become angry for his nephew's sake ﷺ.

THE INTERCESSION TO RAISE THE RANKS OF PEOPLE IN HEAVEN – (Some of the scholars) say this type of intercession is exclusively for the Prophet ﷺ. While (others hold the position) that this (intercession) will be done by him ﷺ and others.

INTERCESSION ON BEHALF OF THOSE WHO COMMITTED MAJOR SINS- This [intercession] is on behalf of the sinners from those who believed in and died upon the true monotheistic creed of Al-Islam. (They are those) who entered the hellfire due to their sins. (There will be an intercession asking) that they be removed from (their punishment). The Messenger of Allah Muhammad ﷺ, other Messengers (peace be upon them all), (as well as) the angels, the righteous, and the martyrs will intercede for that. Likewise, the Qur'an and fasting will be intercessors for their companions (who recited truthfully and sincerely fasted) on the Day of Judgment. Likewise, the children of the believers will be intercessors for their parents.

The Prophetic Fountain

(From faith in the Afterlife) is faith in Al-Hawd: The Fountain of our Prophet Muhammad ﷺ. Its water is whiter than milk, sweeter than honey, and more fragrant than the smell of musk. Whoever takes one drink from it will never be thirsty thereafter.

The Bridge

(From faith in the Afterlife) is faith in As-Siraat: (the Bridge) which is erected over the center of Jahannam (i.e. Hell). People will pass over it (at a speed that is) in accordance with their deeds. So, the first of them (i.e. the fastest of them) will pass over it (at a speed) like that of lightning. Then (there are those who will) pass over it (at a speed) like that of wind. And others will pass over it (at a speed) like that of a bird. All the while the Prophet ﷺ is calling out saying, **"My Lord! Save! Save!"** (This will continue) until the deeds of the slaves would be failing in strength to the point where there will come a man who will not be able to move (across The Bridge) except crawling. On the two sides of the bridge there are hooks that are attached. They are ordered to take certain people. So, there will be those who are injured and cut but safe and those who are cast into and heaped up in the Fire.

We believe in everything that is in the Qur'an and the Sunnah about that Day's events and horrors. May Allah aid us in dealing with them.

Section 8: Faith in Predestination: The Good and the Bad

Faith in Al-Qadaa (i.e. the execution of Allah's Will) and Al-Qadar (i.e. Predestination) - It is to have firm belief that Allah pre-ordained the maqaadeer (i.e. quantities, proportions, measures, numbers, descriptions, lifespan) of His creatures, and that whatever Allah willed occurs, and whatever He did not will, does not transpire. Allah, The Most High, said,

$$ ﴿ إِنَّا كُلَّ شَىْءٍ خَلَقْنَٰهُ بِقَدَرٍ ۝ ﴾ $$

"Verily We have created everything with a qadar (i.e. divine preordainment)" [Al-Qamar: 49]

He, the Most High said,

$$ ﴿ مَّا كَانَ عَلَى ٱلنَّبِيِّ مِنْ حَرَجٍ فِيمَا فَرَضَ ٱللَّهُ لَهُۥ سُنَّةَ ٱللَّهِ فِى ٱلَّذِينَ خَلَوْا۟ مِن قَبْلُ وَكَانَ أَمْرُ ٱللَّهِ قَدَرًا مَّقْدُورًا ۝ ﴾ $$

"And the Command of Allah is a decree determined." [Al-Ahzaab: 38]

The Four Aspects of the Predestination:

1. **Allah's Knowledge** - We believe that Allah (high above and exalted is He) knows all things. He knew what would be and how it would be in His eternal everlasting Knowledge (i.e. His Knowledge which has no beginning or end). So, no new knowledge comes to Him after ignorance, nor does forgetfulness overtake Him after knowledge.[39]

2. **The Writing**- We believe that Allah wrote everything that will happen until The Day of Judgment in Al-Lawh Al-Mahfuth (i.e. The Preserved Tablet).

Allah, the Most High, said,

---

[39] **Translator's Note:** Allah's perfect and complete knowledge is not gained by learning, because He always had knowledge of all things, He was never ignorant or unaware of anything, and Allah never forgets anything ever.

﴿ أَلَمْ تَعْلَمْ أَنَّ ٱللَّهَ يَعْلَمُ مَا فِى ٱلسَّمَآءِ وَٱلْأَرْضِ إِنَّ ذَٰلِكَ فِى كِتَٰبٍ إِنَّ ذَٰلِكَ عَلَى ٱللَّهِ يَسِيرٌ ۝ ﴾

"Don't you know that Allah knows all that is in the heaven and the earth, verily it is all in a book, verily that is easy for Allah." [Al-Hajj: 70]

He, The Most High, said,

﴿ قَالَ فَمَا بَالُ ٱلْقُرُونِ ٱلْأُولَىٰ ۝ قَالَ عِلْمُهَا عِندَ رَبِّى فِى كِتَٰبٍ لَّا يَضِلُّ رَبِّى وَلَا يَنسَى ۝ ﴾

"He (i.e. Pharaoh) said, 'What about the generations of old?' He (i.e. Moses) said, 'The knowledge thereof is with my Lord in a book, my Lord does not err nor does he forget.' [Taa Haa: 51-52]

He (high above and exalted is He) said,

﴿ وَكُلَّ شَىْءٍ أَحْصَيْنَٰهُ فِى إِمَامٍ مُّبِينٍ ۝ ﴾

"And We have taken account of all things in a Clear Book." [Yaa Sin: 12]

Those Things which Enter Under the Aspect of the Writing

- **The Azali (i.e. Eternal) Preordainment**, which took place before the creation of the heavens and the earth, enters under this (aspect of predestination). He (high above and exalted is He) said:

﴿ قُل لَّن يُصِيبَنَآ إِلَّا مَا كَتَبَ ٱللَّهُ لَنَا هُوَ مَوْلَىٰنَا وَعَلَى ٱللَّهِ فَلْيَتَوَكَّلِ ٱلْمُؤْمِنُونَ ۝ ﴾

"Say (Oh Muhammad), 'Nothing will happen to us except that which Allah has written for us.'" [At-Tawbah: 51]

(Also) the writing of the Covenant on the Day [when Allah said:

﴿ أَلَسْتُ بِرَبِّكُمْ ﴾

"Am I not you Lord?"]

Allah, the Most High, said,

﴿ وَإِذْ أَخَذَ رَبُّكَ مِنْ بَنِى ءَادَمَ مِن ظُهُورِهِمْ ذُرِّيَّتَهُمْ وَأَشْهَدَهُمْ عَلَىٰ أَنفُسِهِمْ أَلَسْتُ بِرَبِّكُمْ قَالُوا۟ بَلَىٰ شَهِدْنَا ﴾

"And when your Lord brought forth from the children of Adam, from their loins, their offspring (or from Adam's loins his offspring) and made them testify as to themselves saying (to them), 'Am I not your Lord?' They said, 'Yes, we testify...'" [Al-A'araaf: 172]

- The **Lifetime Preordainment**, when the nutfah (i.e. the mixed male and female sexual fluids) takes form and the angel is sent to blow the spirit into the mudghah (i.e. the embryo) and he (i.e. the angel) is commanded to write four (things about the person who is being formed): their provisions, their lifespan, their deeds, and whether they will be wretched or happy.

- The **Yearly Preordainment**, which takes place in Laylatul-Qadr [a special night that occurs once a year in the Islamic Lunar Month of Ramadan],

Allah, The Most High, said,

$$﴾ فِيهَا يُفْرَقُ كُلُّ أَمْرٍ حَكِيمٍ ٤ ﴿$$

"Therein (that night) is decreed every matter of ordainments."
[Ad-Dukhaan: 4]

Ibn 'Abbaas ﷺ said, **"That which will occur in the (coming) year of death and life and provisions and rain is written from Ummul-Kitaab (i.e. The Mother of The Book, The Preserved Tablet) in Laylatul-Qadr; even those who will make Al-Hajj (that year), it is said so and so will make Al-Hajj and such and such will make Al-Hajj."**

- The **Daily Preordainment** (enters under this aspect).

Allah (high above and exalted is He) said,

$$﴾ كُلَّ يَوْمٍ هُوَ فِي شَأْنٍ ٢٩ ﴿$$

"Every day He has a matter to bring forth." [Ar-Rahmaan: 29]

The Daily Preordainment is a part of the Yearly Preordainment, and the Yearly Preordainment is a part of the Lifetime Preordainment that takes place when the nutfah (i.e. the mixed male and female sexual fluids) takes form, and (that) Lifetime Preordainment is a part of the first Lifetime Preordainment, which took place the Day of The Covenant, and that is a part of The Azali (i.e. Eternal) Preordainment, which The Pen wrote in Al-Imam Al-Mubeen (i.e. The Clear Book, The Preserved Tablet), and Al-Imam Al-Mubeen (i.e. The Clear Book, The Preserved Tablet) is (from) the knowledge of Allah (mighty and majestic is He).

Likewise, in the end, the knowledge of the matters that are pre-ordained is with Allah. So, the first things that were preordained are in His Eternal [Knowledge] (which has no beginning) and the last things that are preordained are in His Everlasting [Knowledge] (which has no end).

$$﴿ وَأَنَّ إِلَىٰ رَبِّكَ ٱلْمُنتَهَىٰ ۝ ﴾$$

"And that to your Lord (Allah) is the End (i.e. return of everything)."
[An-Najm: 42]

3. The Will of Allah

We believe that Allah decreed everything that is in The Heavens and The Earth. There is nothing that exists except by His Will. Whatever He wills comes into existence and whatever He did not will does not come about. Allah said,

$$﴿ إِنَّمَا أَمْرُهُ إِذَآ أَرَادَ شَيْـًٔا أَن يَقُولَ لَهُۥ كُن فَيَكُونُ ۝ ﴾$$

"Verily, His Command, when He intends a thing, is only that He says to it, 'Be!' and then it is!" [Yaa Seen: 82]

He (high above and exalted is He) said,

$$﴿ وَلَوْ شَآءَ ٱللَّهُ مَا ٱقْتَتَلُوا۟ وَلَٰكِنَّ ٱللَّهَ يَفْعَلُ مَا يُرِيدُ ۝ ﴾$$

"...Yet if Allah had willed, they would not have fought one another. But Allah does what He wills."
[Al-Baqarah: 253]

And He (high above and exalted is He) said,

$$﴿ وَلَوْ شَآءَ ٱللَّهُ لَجَمَعَهُمْ عَلَى ٱلْهُدَىٰ ﴾$$

"...Had Allah so willed, He could have guided them all...." [Al-An'aam: 35]

And He (high above and exalted is He) said,

$$﴿ وَلَوْ شَآءَ رَبُّكَ لَجَعَلَ ٱلنَّاسَ أُمَّةً وَٰحِدَةً وَلَا يَزَالُونَ مُخْتَلِفِينَ ۝ ﴾$$

"And if your Lord had so willed, He could surely have made mankind one Ummah (i.e. one nation following one religion), but they will not cease to disagree." [Hud: 118]

Allah, the Most High said,

63

﴿ وَلَوْ شِئْنَا لَآتَيْنَا كُلَّ نَفْسٍ هُدَىٰهَا وَلَٰكِنْ حَقَّ ٱلْقَوْلُ مِنِّى ﴾

"And if We had willed, surely We would have given every person his guidance, but the Word from Me took effect..." [As- Sajdah: 13]

Allah, the Most High, said,

﴿ أَوَلَمْ يَسِيرُوا۟ فِى ٱلْأَرْضِ فَيَنظُرُوا۟ كَيْفَ كَانَ عَٰقِبَةُ ٱلَّذِينَ مِن قَبْلِهِمْ وَكَانُوٓا۟ أَشَدَّ مِنْهُمْ قُوَّةً وَمَا كَانَ ٱللَّهُ لِيُعْجِزَهُۥ مِن شَىْءٍ فِى ٱلسَّمَٰوَٰتِ وَلَا فِى ٱلْأَرْضِ إِنَّهُۥ كَانَ عَلِيمًا قَدِيرًا ۝ ﴾

"Have they not travelled throughout the land to see what was the end of those ⸢destroyed⸣ before them? They were far superior in might. But there is nothing that can escape Allah in the heavens or the earth. He is certainly All-Knowing, Most Capable." [Faatir: 44]

4. The Aspect of Creation

Allah, the All-Mighty God, creates every doer and his actions. He creates everything that moves and its movement. And He creates everything that is unmoving and its stillness. He, the Most High, said,

﴿ وَٱللَّهُ خَلَقَكُمْ وَمَا تَعْمَلُونَ ۝ ﴾

"While Allah has created you and what you make!" [As- Saaffaat: 96]

And He said,

﴿ ٱللَّهُ خَٰلِقُ كُلِّ شَىْءٍ وَهُوَ عَلَىٰ كُلِّ شَىْءٍ وَكِيلٌ ۝ ﴾

"Allah is the Creator of all things, and He is the Wakeel (i.e. Trustee, Disposer of affairs, Guardian, etc.) over all things." [Az-Zumar: 62]

The Actions of the Servants

We believe, along with the previous points, that the servants have ability to do their deeds. They have volition and will. Allah (high above and exalted is He) is their Creator and the Creator of their wills, abilities, statements, and actions. The statements and deeds, which come from them, are truly attributed to them. And they will be rewarded or punished (in accordance to these deeds and actions). (The servants) are not able to do anything except that which Allah made them able to do. They cannot do anything unless Allah (high above and exalted is He) willed it. Allah said,

﴿ إِنَّ هَٰذِهِۦ تَذْكِرَةٌ فَمَن شَآءَ ٱتَّخَذَ إِلَىٰ رَبِّهِۦ سَبِيلًا ۝ وَمَا تَشَآءُونَ إِلَّآ أَن يَشَآءَ ٱللَّهُ إِنَّ ٱللَّهَ كَانَ عَلِيمًا حَكِيمًا ۝ ﴾

64

"Verily! This (i.e. these verses of Al-Qur'aan) is an admonition, so whosoever wills, let him take a Path to his Lord. But you cannot will, unless Allah wills. Verily, Allah is Ever All-Knowing, All-Wise." [Al-Insaan: 29-30]

And He said,

﴿ إِنْ هُوَ إِلَّا ذِكْرٌ لِّلْعَٰلَمِينَ ۝ لِمَن شَآءَ مِنكُمْ أَن يَسْتَقِيمَ ۝ وَمَا تَشَآءُونَ إِلَّا أَن يَشَآءَ اللَّهُ رَبُّ الْعَٰلَمِينَ ۝ ﴾

"Verily, this (i.e. The Qur'aan) is no less than a Reminder to (all) the 'Aalameen (i.e. Mankind and Jinns). To whomsoever among you who wills to walk straight, and you will not, unless (it be) that Allah wills, the Lord of the 'Aalameen (i.e. the Worlds; Mankind, Jinns, and all that exists)." [At-Takweer: 27-29]

Allah, the All-Mighty, said,

﴿ لَا يُكَلِّفُ اللَّهُ نَفْسًا إِلَّا وُسْعَهَا لَهَا مَا كَسَبَتْ وَعَلَيْهَا مَا اكْتَسَبَتْ ﴾

"Allah does not burden a soul beyond its ability. It gets reward for that (good) which it has earned, and it is punished for that (evil) which it has earned..." [Al-Baqarah: 286]

And He (high above and exalted is He) said,

﴿ وَتِلْكَ الْجَنَّةُ الَّتِي أُورِثْتُمُوهَا بِمَا كُنتُمْ تَعْمَلُونَ ۝ ﴾

"This is the Paradise which you have been made to inherit because of what you used to do." [Az-Zukhruf: 72]

Meaning: because of the actions and (deeds) you used to do. Allah, the Most High said,

﴿ وَذُوقُوا عَذَابَ الْخُلْدِ بِمَا كُنتُمْ تَعْمَلُونَ ۝ ﴾

"...And taste the everlasting punishment because of what you used to do." [As-Sajdah: 14]

And He (high above and exalted is He) said,

﴿ فَمَن يَعْمَلْ مِثْقَالَ ذَرَّةٍ خَيْرًا يَرَهُ ۝ وَمَن يَعْمَلْ مِثْقَالَ ذَرَّةٍ شَرًّا يَرَهُ ۝ ﴾

"So whosoever does good equal to the weight of a dharrah (i.e. the smallest ant), shall see it. And whosoever does evil equal to the weight of a dharrah (i.e. the smallest ant), shall see it." [Az-Zalzalah:7-8]

65

Preordainment should not Prohibit One from Taking the Means nor Does it Obligate Neglecting Them

We believe that preordainment should not prohibit a person from taking the means and does not obligate neglecting them. That is why when the Prophet 變 informed his Companions about (the fact that) matters are preordained and that they will occur, and (he mentioned) about the drying up of The Pen, it was said to him, **"Shall we not then be reliant on what is written for us and leave off work (i.e. taking the means)?"** He said, **"No! Work, for verily it is made easy for everyone (i.e. it is made easy for everyone to do that which they were created for)."** Then he 變 recited,

$$﴿ فَأَمَّا مَنْ أَعْطَىٰ وَٱتَّقَىٰ ۞ وَصَدَّقَ بِٱلْحُسْنَىٰ ۞ فَسَنُيَسِّرُهُ لِلْيُسْرَىٰ ۞ وَأَمَّا مَنْ بَخِلَ وَٱسْتَغْنَىٰ ۞ وَكَذَّبَ بِٱلْحُسْنَىٰ ۞ فَسَنُيَسِّرُهُ لِلْعُسْرَىٰ ۞ ﴾$$

"As for him who gives (in charity) and keeps his duty to Allah and fears Him, and believes in Al-Husna[40] (i.e. The Best), We will make smooth for him the path of ease (i.e. goodness). But he who is miserly and thinks himself self-sufficient, and rejects Al-Husna[41] (i.e. The Best); We will make smooth for him the path of difficulty (i.e. evil)." [Al-Layl: 5-10]

Thus, the preordained matters have means that lead to them. Just as getting married is the means for (the attainment of) children and tilling is a reason for the presence of crops. Likewise, good deeds are a means to enter Al-Jennah (i.e. The Garden, Heaven) and bad deeds are a means to enter An-Naar (i.e. the Fire, Hell).

---

[40] **Translator's Note:** Al-Imam As-Sa'dee says in his Tafsir in explanation of this, "Meaning: the one who believes in [the statement] laa ilaaha illa Allah (i.e. There is no true God except Allah or none has the right or deserves to be worshipped except Allah) and all that it indicates of all the beliefs of the religion and that which results from them of compensation in The Afterlife."

[41] **Translator's Note:** As-Sa'dee says in his Tafsir in explanation of this, "Meaning: (the one who rejects) what Allah obligated the slaves to believe in of good beliefs."

Section 9: The Correct Creed Concerning Al-Iman (Faith)

From the totality of the creed of Ahlus-Sunnah is to believe that true faith is comprised of **speech of the tongue**, that one pronounces the testimony of At-Tawhid that there is no deity (deserving of worship) except Allah and that Muhammad is the Messenger of Allah ﷺ. (It includes) **belief in the heart**: which is that one is completely certain of the truthfulness of the declaration of At-Tawhid. Last, (faith is) **actions with the limbs**.

Al-Imam Ash-Shaafi'ee (may Allah have mercy on him) said, "**It was the consensus among the companions, those who followed them, those who came after them, and those who we met that they would say, 'Al-Iman (i.e. Faith) is speech, action, and intention. And one of these three by itself does not suffice without the others.'**" Al-Laalakaaee narrated it in *As-Sunnah.*

The Increasing and Decreasing of Al-Iman

Al-Iman (i.e. Faith) increases due to obedience (i.e. good deeds) and decreases due to disobedience (i.e. sins). He (high above and exalted is He) said,

$$﴿ ٱلَّذِينَ قَالَ لَهُمُ ٱلنَّاسُ إِنَّ ٱلنَّاسَ قَدْ جَمَعُواْ لَكُمْ فَٱخْشَوْهُمْ فَزَادَهُمْ إِيمَٰنًا وَقَالُواْ حَسْبُنَا ٱللَّهُ وَنِعْمَ ٱلْوَكِيلُ ۝ ﴾$$

"Those (i.e. believers) unto whom the people (i.e. the hypocrites) said, 'Verily, the people (i.e. the pagans) have gathered against you (i.e. they have gathered against you a great army), therefore, fear them.' But it (only) increased them in Iman (i.e. Faith), and they said: 'Allah (Alone) is Sufficient for us, and He is the Best Disposer of affairs.'" [Aal-'Imraan: 173]

And He (high above and exalted is He) said,

$$﴿ وَإِذَا تُلِيَتْ عَلَيْهِمْ ءَايَٰتُهُۥ زَادَتْهُمْ إِيمَٰنًا وَعَلَىٰ رَبِّهِمْ يَتَوَكَّلُونَ ۝ ﴾$$

"...And when His Verses (i.e. this Qur'aan) are recited unto them, they (i.e. the Verses) increase their Faith; and they put their trust in their Lord (Alone)." [Al-Anfaal: 2]

And He, The Most High said,

﴿ وَإِذَا مَآ أُنزِلَتْ سُورَةٌ فَمِنْهُم مَّن يَقُولُ أَيُّكُمْ زَادَتْهُ هَـٰذِهِۦ إِيمَـٰنًا فَأَمَّا ٱلَّذِينَ ءَامَنُوا۟ فَزَادَتْهُمْ إِيمَـٰنًا وَهُمْ يَسْتَبْشِرُونَ ﴿١٢٤﴾ ﴾

"And whenever there comes down a Surah (i.e. chapter from The Qur'an), some of them (i.e. the hypocrites) say, 'Which of you has had his Iman (i.e. Faith) increased by it?' As for those who believe, it has increased their Iman (i.e. Faith), and they rejoice." [At-Tawbah: 124]

And He (high above and exalted is He) said,

﴿ وَلَمَّا رَءَا ٱلْمُؤْمِنُونَ ٱلْأَحْزَابَ قَالُوا۟ هَـٰذَا مَا وَعَدَنَا ٱللَّهُ وَرَسُولُهُۥ وَصَدَقَ ٱللَّهُ وَرَسُولُهُۥ وَمَا زَادَهُمْ إِلَّآ إِيمَـٰنًا وَتَسْلِيمًا ﴿٢٢﴾ ﴾

"And when the believers saw Al-Ahzaab (i.e. the Confederates), they said: „This is what Allah and His Messenger had promised us; and Allah and His Messenger had spoken the truth.' And it only added to their faith and to their submissiveness (i.e. their submissiveness to Allah)." [Al-Ahzaab: 22]

And He (high above and exalted is He) said,

﴿ هُوَ ٱلَّذِىٓ أَنزَلَ ٱلسَّكِينَةَ فِى قُلُوبِ ٱلْمُؤْمِنِينَ لِيَزْدَادُوٓا۟ إِيمَـٰنًا مَّعَ إِيمَـٰنِهِمْ وَلِلَّهِ جُنُودُ ٱلسَّمَـٰوَٰتِ وَٱلْأَرْضِ وَكَانَ ٱللَّهُ عَلِيمًا حَكِيمًا ﴿٤﴾ ﴾

"He is the One Who sent down serenity upon the hearts of the believers so that they may increase even more in their faith. To Allah ˹alone˺ belong the forces of the heavens and the earth. And Allah is All-Knowing, All-Wise." [Al-Fath:4]

Allah, the Most High, said

﴿ وَيَزْدَادَ ٱلَّذِينَ ءَامَنُوٓا۟ إِيمَـٰنًا﴾

"...And (in order that) the believers may increase in Iman (i.e. Faith) ..." [Al-Muddaththir: 31]

[It is narrated] in Sahih Al-Bukhari and Sahih Muslim, on the authority of Abdullah bin 'Umar ﷺ, that the Prophet ﷺ admonished the women and he said to them, "I have not seen anyone deficient in intelligence and religion who could make a strong-willed man lose his intellect more than one of you." So, this is proof that Al-Iman (i.e. Faith) decreases. Similarly, is his ﷺ statement, "The most complete of believers in Iman (i.e. Faith) are those who have the best character (**manners**)." Imam Ahmad and others narrated (this hadith) on the authority of Abu Hurairah. Therefore, if the one who is described as having good character is the most complete of believers in Iman (i.e. Faith), then other than him, whose character is poor, has less Iman (i.e. Faith).

Al-Iman is not without Conviction

Al-Iman (i.e. Faith) is not (just) statements and actions without conviction (in the heart), for this is the faith of the hypocrites. Allah (high above and exalted is He) said,

﴿ وَمِنَ ٱلنَّاسِ مَن يَقُولُ ءَامَنَّا بِٱللَّهِ وَبِٱلْيَوْمِ ٱلْأَخِرِ وَمَا هُم بِمُؤْمِنِينَ ۝ ﴾

"And of mankind, there are some who say, 'We believe in Allah and the Last Day.' While in fact they do not believe." [Al- Baqarah: 8]

Al-Iman is not Just Having the Knowledge

Al-Iman (i.e. Faith) is not just having the knowledge, because that is the Iman of the disbelievers and those who make juhood (i.e. reject, while knowing the truth). Allah, the All-Mighty, said,

﴿ وَجَحَدُواْ بِهَا وَٱسْتَيْقَنَتْهَآ أَنفُسُهُمْ ظُلْمًا وَعُلُوًّا ﴾

"And, although their hearts were convinced the signs were true, they still denied them wrongfully and arrogantly...." [An-Naml: 14]

And He (high above and exalted is He) said,

﴿ قَدْ نَعْلَمُ إِنَّهُۥ لَيَحْزُنُكَ ٱلَّذِى يَقُولُونَ فَإِنَّهُمْ لَا يُكَذِّبُونَكَ وَلَـٰكِنَّ ٱلظَّـٰلِمِينَ بِـَٔايَـٰتِ ٱللَّهِ يَجْحَدُونَ ۝ ﴾

"We certainly know that what they say grieves you ˹O Prophet˺. It is not your honesty they question—it is Allah's signs that the wrongdoers deny." [Al-An'aam: 33]

And He (high above and exalted is He) said,

﴿ ٱلَّذِينَ ءَاتَيْنَـٰهُمُ ٱلْكِتَـٰبَ يَعْرِفُونَهُۥ كَمَا يَعْرِفُونَ أَبْنَآءَهُمْ وَإِنَّ فَرِيقًا مِّنْهُمْ لَيَكْتُمُونَ ٱلْحَقَّ وَهُمْ يَعْلَمُونَ ۝ ﴾

"Those to whom We gave the Scripture to (i.e. the Jews and Christians) recognize him (i.e. Muhammad ﷺ or the Ka'bah at Makkah) as they recognize their sons." [Al-Baqarah: 146]

He (high above and exalted is He) said,

﴿ فَلَمَّا جَآءَهُم مَّا عَرَفُواْ كَفَرُواْ بِهِۦ فَلَعْنَةُ ٱللَّهِ عَلَى ٱلْكَٰفِرِينَ ۝ ﴾

"...Then when there came to them that which they had recognized, they disbelieved in it." [Al-Baqarah: 89]

And He (high above and exalted is He) said,

﴿ وَعَادًا وَثَمُودَاْ وَقَد تَّبَيَّنَ لَكُم مِّن مَّسَٰكِنِهِمْ وَزَيَّنَ لَهُمُ ٱلشَّيْطَٰنُ أَعْمَٰلَهُمْ فَصَدَّهُمْ عَنِ ٱلسَّبِيلِ وَكَانُواْ مُسْتَبْصِرِينَ ۝ ﴾

"And 'Aad and Thamud (people)! And indeed (their destruction) is clearly apparent to you from their (ruined) dwellings. Satan made their deeds seem fair to them, and turned them away from the (Right) Path, though they were mustabsirun (i.e. intelligent)." [Al-'Ankabut: 38]

Al-Iman is not Without Action

Al-Iman is not speech and conviction without deeds, for Allah called (good) deeds Iman (i.e. faith). Hence, He (high above and exalted is He) said,

﴿ وَمَا كَانَ ٱللَّهُ لِيُضِيعَ إِيمَٰنَكُمْ ﴾

"And Allah would never make your Iman (i.e. faith) to be lost." [Al-Baqarah:143]

This means: (He will not make) your prayers towards Jerusalem lost (i.e. the prayers that they did before the verse commanding them to turn towards The Ka'bah was revealed). (It is narrated) in Bukhari and Muslim from the narration of Ibn 'Abbaas that the Prophet ﷺ said to the delegation of 'Abdul Qays, **"I order you with four things: to have Al-Iman (i.e. Faith) in Allah. Do you know what Al-Iman (i.e. Faith) in Allah is? It is to testify that there is no true God except Allah, and none truly deserves to be worshipped except Him, to establish the Salat (i.e. the five daily prayers), to give the Zakat (i.e. a fixed annual charity), to fast in Ramadan, and that you give a fifth of your spoils of war."** Also, in Bukhari and Muslim it is narrated on the authority of Abu Hurairah ﷺ that the Messenger of Allah ﷺ said, **"Al-Iman is seventy some or sixty some odd branches. The best of which is the statement laa ilaaha illa Allah and the lowest of them is removing some harmful obstruction from the road. And shyness is also a branch of Al-Iman."**

The Ruling Regarding Deeds

There is no action, which if it is abandoned, is disbelief except the Salat (i.e. the five daily prayers). So, whoever abandons it completely then he has disbelieved. The Companions of The Messenger of Allah ﷺ had a consensus about this. 'Abdullah bin Shaqeeq said, **"The Companions of The Messenger of Allah ﷺ did not see the abandonment of any action as being disbelief except (for the abandonment of) the Salat."**[42]

The Ruling Regarding Declaring Someone to be a Disbeliever

At-Takfeer (i.e. declaring someone to be a disbeliever) is a right that belongs to Allah (alone). No one is declared to be a disbeliever except he who Allah or His Messenger ﷺ declares to be a disbeliever, or he who the Muslims have a consensus about declaring to be a disbeliever. Whoever declares someone to be a disbeliever for a reason that does not have a clear proof from the Qur'an, the authentic Sunnah, or the consensus of the Muslims, then he deserves to be punished and reprimanded harshly. This is because, **"Whoever accuses a believer of kufr (i.e. disbelief) then it is like killing him."** This is narrated in Al-Bukhari on the authority of Thabit Ibn Ad-Dahhaak from The Prophet ﷺ.

Kufr occurs by a statement of disbelief, of which there is no reasonable difference of opinion about (it being a statement of disbelief). The same is the case for actions and beliefs (of kufr). Al-Istihlal (i.e. declaring that which Allah made prohibited to be permissible) is not a pre-condition for disbelief (to occur). And there is a difference between a general pronouncement of takfeer (i.e. saying in general that whoever does or believes or says such and such is a disbeliever) and making takfeer of a specific person (i.e. declaring a specific person a disbeliever). A general takfeer is like a general threat (by Allah); it is necessary to speak generally concerning it. For instance, the statement of the Imams (i.e. the Scholars), **"Whoever says The Qur'an is created is a kaafir (i.e. disbeliever)."** And like the statement of Ibn Khuzaymah (may Allah have mercy on him), **"Whoever does not confirm that Allah is above His Throne; He is ascended above His Seven Heavens, then he is a kaafir (i.e. disbeliever); his blood is permissible (to shed) and his wealth is spoils of war (i.e. to be donated to the Muslim treasury)."**

To declare a specific person to be a kaafir (i.e. disbeliever) it is necessary that the pre-conditions are fulfilled and those things that would obstruct (one from being called a disbeliever) are negated. Thus, it is not necessary that from a general takfeer that a specific person is made takfeer of (i.e. declared to be a disbeliever), until the pre-conditions of takfeer are fulfilled and those things that would obstruct it from occurring have been negated.

---

[42] Collected by At-Tirmidhi

Section 10: The Correct Creed Concerning the Status of Those Who Commit Major Sins

From the totality of the creed of Ahlus-Sunnah wal Jamaa'ah is that none of the sins, other than shirk (i.e. ascribing partners to Allah), remove the Muslim from the religion of Al-Islam; except if he regards (sins) to be halaal (i.e. lawful or permissible to do). This is the case whether he commits the sin while believing it to be permissible, or (even if) he believes it to be lawful but does not commit the sin. This is because (if he deemed it lawful) he would be rejecting the Book (i.e. The Qur'an) and the Messenger ﷺ. This is disbelief in the Book (i.e. The Qur'an), the Sunnah, and the ijmaa' (i.e. consensus). No sin that is less than shirk will cause anyone to dwell eternally in the fire of Hell. As Allah says,

﴿ إِنَّ ٱللَّهَ لَا يَغْفِرُ أَن يُشْرَكَ بِهِۦ وَيَغْفِرُ مَا دُونَ ذَٰلِكَ لِمَن يَشَآءُ ﴾

"Indeed, Allah does not forgive associating others with Him ˹in worship˺, but forgives anything else of whoever He wills...." [An-Nisaa': 48]

This verse states that sinful person is left to Allah's Will ﷻ. If He (high above and exalted, is He) wills, He may pardon him by His graciousness and generosity. And if He wills, He may enter him into the Fire (for a time that is) in accordance with the amount of his sins, as a (means of purification and atonement). Then He will take him out of (the hellfire) on account of the sinners belief in the oneness of Allah.

The Sinner is Deficient in Faith

Allah mentioned some of the major sins like murder and transgression in His Book (i.e. The Qur'an). He confirmed that those (Muslims commit these atrocities still) have (a level of faith).[43] They are believers on account of their

---

[43] **Translator's Note:** Let the new Muslim or non-Muslim reader be aware that the point the author is making here is not that Islam sees these terrible deeds as being

72

Iman. While simultaneously, they are wicked sinners due to their disobedience. He (high above and exalted is He) said,

$$\text{﴾ يَـٰٓأَيُّهَا ٱلَّذِينَ ءَامَنُواْ كُتِبَ عَلَيۡكُمُ ٱلۡقِصَاصُ فِى ٱلۡقَتۡلَىۖ ٱلۡحُرُّ بِٱلۡحُرِّ وَٱلۡعَبۡدُ بِٱلۡعَبۡدِ وَٱلۡأُنثَىٰ بِٱلۡأُنثَىٰۚ فَمَنۡ عُفِىَ لَهُۥ مِنۡ أَخِيهِ شَىۡءٌ فَٱتِّبَاعُۢ بِٱلۡمَعۡرُوفِ وَأَدَآءٌ إِلَيۡهِ بِإِحۡسَـٰنٍۗ ذَٰلِكَ تَخۡفِيفٌ مِّن رَّبِّكُمۡ وَرَحۡمَةٌۗ فَمَنِ ٱعۡتَدَىٰ بَعۡدَ ذَٰلِكَ فَلَهُۥ عَذَابٌ أَلِيمٌ ﴿٧٨﴾ ﴾}$$

"O believers! The law of retaliation is set for you in cases of murder—a free man for a free man, a slave for a slave, and a female for a female.I But if the offender is pardoned by the victim's guardian, then blood-money should be decided fairly and payment should be made courteously. This is a concession and a mercy from your Lord. But whoever transgresses after that will suffer a painful punishment." [Al-Baqarah:178]

Allah, The Most High, confirmed that both the killer *and* the killed from the believers have Iman; and confirmed for them both the brotherhood of Al-Iman.

A Person can be called a Faasiq and a Muslim without Contradiction

There is no contradiction between deeming a deed and its doer to be evil, while considering such a person to be Muslim and even interacting with them with the applicable Islamic etiquettes and rights unique to the Muslims. The story of Abdullah Himaar, reported by Bukhari in his authentic collection, clarifies this to the utmost extent. Abdullah Himaar drank some alcohol. He was then taken to The Prophet ﷺ. Whereupon one of the Companions ﷺ said, "May Allah curse him! How often he is brought!" The Prophet ﷺ said, "Do not curse him, for indeed he loves Allah and His Messenger ﷺ." So, 'Abdullah Himaar did not exit Al-Islam because of this major sin. Rather the Prophet ﷺ affirmed that he had Faith, even though he committed this major sin.

The Categories of Kufr & Shirk

The explanation of this (grouping) is that each of the (following) terms, Kufr (i.e. disbelief), shirk (i.e. polytheism, ascribing partners to Allah), thulm (i.e. wrongdoing or oppression), fisq (i.e. evildoing), and nifaaq (i.e. hypocrisy), are all divided into two categories in the Islamic law:

---

something light. Rather, the point is that the believer who does these types of deeds that are less than the major disbelief and polytheism can still have *some* faith. Though they would be severely deficient in their commitment to the religion.

73

1. **Major-** This (type) removes a person from the fold of Islam because it violates the foundation of the religion.
2. **Minor-** This (type) reduces the completeness of faith. It does not take a person out of the fold of Islam. This is the categorization of the Salaf (i.e. the predecessors, the companions and those who learned from them and those who learned from their students, the early generations of Muslim scholars upon the Prophetic Way). The scholar of this ummah, and the explainer of The Qur'an, Ibn 'Abbaas, confirmed that there is a type of kufr (i.e. disbelief) that is less than (true) Kufr (i.e. the major disbelief), a type of thulm (i.e. wrongdoing, injustice) that is less than (the major type of) Thulm, a type of fusooq (i.e. sinfulness) that is less than (the major) Fusooq, and a type of nifaaq (i.e. hypocrisy) that is less than (the major type of) Nifaaq.

Major Kufr

Allah termed the one who invokes other than Him a **kaafir** (i.e. disbeliever), a **mushrik** (i.e. one who deifies or worships other than Allah or associates anything with Allah), and a **thaalim** (i.e. wrongdoer or oppressor). Allah, the Most High, said,

$$﴿ وَمَن يَدْعُ مَعَ ٱللَّهِ إِلَٰهًا ءَاخَرَ لَا بُرْهَٰنَ لَهُۥ بِهِۦ فَإِنَّمَا حِسَابُهُۥ عِندَ رَبِّهِۦٓ إِنَّهُۥ لَا يُفْلِحُ ٱلْكَٰفِرُونَ ۝ ﴾$$

"Whoever invokes, besides Allah, another god—for which they can have no proof—they will surely find their penalty with their Lord. Indeed, the disbelievers will never succeed." [Al-Mu'minoon:117]

And He (high above and exalted is He) said,

$$﴿ قُلْ إِنَّمَآ أَدْعُواْ رَبِّي وَلَآ أُشْرِكُ بِهِۦٓ أَحَدًا ۝ ﴾$$

"Say, ˹O Prophet,˺ "I call only upon my Lord, associating none with Him ˹in worship˺."" [Al-Jinn: 20]

And He, the Most High, said,

$$﴿ وَلَا تَدْعُ مِن دُونِ ٱللَّهِ مَا لَا يَنفَعُكَ وَلَا يَضُرُّكَ فَإِن فَعَلْتَ فَإِنَّكَ إِذًا مِّنَ ٱلظَّٰلِمِينَ ۝ ﴾$$

"And invoke not other than Allah that which will neither benefit you nor harm you, but if you were to do so then you would certainly be one of the thaalimoon (i.e. wrongdoers)." [Yunus: 106]

And He (high above and exalted is He) said,

$$﴿ إِلَّآ إِبْلِيسَ كَانَ مِنَ ٱلْجِنِّ فَفَسَقَ عَنْ أَمْرِ رَبِّهِ ﴾$$

"...Except Iblees (i.e. Satan). He was one of the jinn, he fasaqa (i.e. rebelled) against the Command of his Lord." [Al-Kahf: 50]

(These verses) are all concerning major kufr, shirk, oppression, and wickedness., the type which does not mix with Iman.

Minor Kufr

Allah said,

$$﴿ وَمَن لَّمْ يَحْكُم بِمَآ أَنزَلَ ٱللَّهُ فَأُوْلَٰٓئِكَ هُمُ ٱلْكَٰفِرُونَ ﴾$$

"...And whosoever does not judge by what Allah has revealed, such are the kaafiroon (i.e. disbelievers)." [Al-Maa'idah: 44]

And He said,

$$﴿ وَمَن لَّمْ يَحْكُم بِمَآ أَنزَلَ ٱللَّهُ فَأُوْلَٰٓئِكَ هُمُ ٱلظَّٰلِمُونَ ﴾$$

"...And whosoever does not judge by what Allah revealed, such are the thaalimoon (i.e. the wrongdoers)." [Al-Maa'idah:45]

And He (high above and exalted is He) said,

$$﴿ وَمَن لَّمْ يَحْكُم بِمَآ أَنزَلَ ٱللَّهُ فَأُوْلَٰٓئِكَ هُمُ ٱلْفَٰسِقُونَ ﴾$$

"...And whosoever does not judge by what Allah revealed, such are the faasiqoon (i.e. the rebellious, those who leave obedience)." [Al-Maa'idah: 47]

And Allah (high above and exalted is He) said:

$$﴿ إِنَّ ٱلَّذِينَ يَأْكُلُونَ أَمْوَٰلَ ٱلْيَتَٰمَىٰ ظُلْمًا إِنَّمَا يَأْكُلُونَ فِى بُطُونِهِمْ نَارًا وَسَيَصْلَوْنَ سَعِيرًا ﴾$$

"Verily, those who unjustly eat up the property of orphans, they eat up only a fire into their bellies, and they will be burnt in the blazing Fire!" [An-Nisaa: 10]

The Prophet ﷺ said, "Insulting a Muslim is wickedness and fighting him is disbelief." He ﷺ also said, "Whosoever swears by other than Allah then he has disbelieved or committed polytheism."

Section 11: The Correct Creed Concerning the Companions of the Messenger of Allah ﷺ

From the beliefs of Ahlus-Sunnah wal Jamaa'ah is having love for the Companions of the Messenger of Allah ﷺ, being loyal to them, asking Allah to be pleased with them and to forgive them, and commending them. Allah ﷻ said,

﴿ وَٱلسَّٰبِقُونَ ٱلۡأَوَّلُونَ مِنَ ٱلۡمُهَٰجِرِينَ وَٱلۡأَنصَارِ وَٱلَّذِينَ ٱتَّبَعُوهُم بِإِحۡسَٰنٍ رَّضِيَ ٱللَّهُ عَنۡهُمۡ وَرَضُواْ عَنۡهُ وَأَعَدَّ لَهُمۡ جَنَّٰتٍ تَجۡرِي تَحۡتَهَا ٱلۡأَنۡهَٰرُ خَٰلِدِينَ فِيهَآ أَبَدٗاۚ ذَٰلِكَ ٱلۡفَوۡزُ ٱلۡعَظِيمُ ۝ ﴾

"As for the foremost—the first of the Emigrants and the Helpers—and those who follow them in ihsaan (i.e. goodness), Allah is pleased with them and they are pleased with Him. And He has prepared for them Gardens under which rivers flow, to stay there for ever and ever. That is the ultimate triumph." [At-Tawbah: 100]

So, Allah's pleasure with the foremost believers (i.e. the companions) is without Him having made Al-Ihsaan a condition (i.e. because they are already upon goodness to begin with) a condition on them. While He is not pleased with those who follow them unless they follow them with Al-Ihsaan (i.e. exactness). And He ﷻ said,

﴿ ۞ لَّقَدۡ رَضِيَ ٱللَّهُ عَنِ ٱلۡمُؤۡمِنِينَ إِذۡ يُبَايِعُونَكَ تَحۡتَ ٱلشَّجَرَةِ فَعَلِمَ مَا فِي قُلُوبِهِمۡ فَأَنزَلَ ٱلسَّكِينَةَ عَلَيۡهِمۡ وَأَثَٰبَهُمۡ فَتۡحٗا قَرِيبٗا ۝ ﴾

"Indeed, Allah was pleased with the believers when they gave the pledge to you (Oh Muhammad) under the tree: He knew what was in their hearts, and He sent down As-Sakeenah (i.e. calmness and tranquility) upon them, and He rewarded them with a near victory." [Al-Fath: 18]

Whosoever Allah is pleased with, He will never be angry with ever. It is confirmed in the authentic hadith that the Prophet ﷺ said, "No one will enter the Fire who gave the pledge under the tree."⁴⁴

The Virtues of the Muhaajiroon⁴⁵

Allah mentioned the Muhaajiroon and described them as being the truthful ones. He ﷺ said,

﴿ لِلْفُقَرَآءِ ٱلْمُهَٰجِرِينَ ٱلَّذِينَ أُخْرِجُواْ مِن دِيَٰرِهِمْ وَأَمْوَٰلِهِمْ يَبْتَغُونَ فَضْلًا مِّنَ ٱللَّهِ وَرِضْوَٰنًا وَيَنصُرُونَ ٱللَّهَ وَرَسُولَهُۥٓ أُوْلَٰٓئِكَ هُمُ ٱلصَّٰدِقُونَ ۝ ﴾

"'Some of the gains will be' for poor emigrants who were driven out of their homes and wealth, seeking Allah's bounty and pleasure, and standing up for Allah and His Messenger. They are the ones true in faith." [Al-Hashr: 8]

The Virtue of the Ansar⁴⁶

Then Allah ﷺ mentioned the Ansaar and said,

﴿ وَٱلَّذِينَ تَبَوَّءُو ٱلدَّارَ وَٱلْإِيمَٰنَ مِن قَبْلِهِمْ يُحِبُّونَ مَنْ هَاجَرَ إِلَيْهِمْ وَلَا يَجِدُونَ فِى صُدُورِهِمْ حَاجَةً مِّمَّآ أُوتُواْ وَيُؤْثِرُونَ عَلَىٰٓ أَنفُسِهِمْ وَلَوْ كَانَ بِهِمْ خَصَاصَةٌ وَمَن يُوقَ شُحَّ نَفْسِهِۦ فَأُوْلَٰٓئِكَ هُمُ ٱلْمُفْلِحُونَ ۝ ﴾

"And (it is also for) those who, before them, had homes (in Al- Madinah) and had adopted the Faith, love those who emigrate to them, and have no jealousy in their chests for that which they have been given (i.e. for that which the emigrants have been given from the booty of Banu An-Nadeer), and give them (i.e. the Muhaajiroon) preference over themselves even though they themselves were in need of that. And whosoever is saved from his own covetousness, such are they who will be successful." [Al-Hashr: 9]

Then Allah ﷺ mentioned the status of those believers who come after them, those who follow the companions of the Messenger of Allah ﷺ with Al-Ihsaan (i.e. in goodness or with exactness). He ﷺ said,

﴿ وَٱلَّذِينَ جَآءُو مِنۢ بَعْدِهِمْ يَقُولُونَ رَبَّنَا ٱغْفِرْ لَنَا وَلِإِخْوَٰنِنَا ٱلَّذِينَ سَبَقُونَا بِٱلْإِيمَٰنِ وَلَا تَجْعَلْ فِى قُلُوبِنَا غِلًّا لِّلَّذِينَ ءَامَنُواْ رَبَّنَآ إِنَّكَ رَءُوفٌ رَّحِيمٌ ۝ ﴾

"And those who came after them say, 'Our Lord forgive us and our brothers

---

⁴⁴ Collected by At-Tirmidhi, Ahmad, and authenticated by Al-Albani in Sahih Abu Dawud from the hadith of Jabir bin Abdullah
⁴⁵**Translator's Note:** Those Companions who migrated from Mekkah to Madinah.
⁴⁶**Translator's Note:** Those Companions who inhabited Madinah and helped the Muhaajiroon Who Came to Them

who preceded us in Faith, and put not in our hearts any hatred against those who have believed. Our Lord you are indeed full of kindness, Most Merciful.'" [Al-Hashr: 10]

And He (ﷺ) said,

> ﴿ مُّحَمَّدٌ رَّسُولُ ٱللَّهِ وَٱلَّذِينَ مَعَهُۥٓ أَشِدَّآءُ عَلَى ٱلْكُفَّارِ رُحَمَآءُ بَيْنَهُمْ تَرَىٰهُمْ رُكَّعًا سُجَّدًا يَبْتَغُونَ فَضْلًا مِّنَ ٱللَّهِ وَرِضْوَٰنًا سِيمَاهُمْ فِى وُجُوهِهِم مِّنْ أَثَرِ ٱلسُّجُودِ ذَٰلِكَ مَثَلُهُمْ فِى ٱلتَّوْرَىٰةِ وَمَثَلُهُمْ فِى ٱلْإِنجِيلِ كَزَرْعٍ أَخْرَجَ شَطْـَٔهُۥ فَـَٔازَرَهُۥ فَٱسْتَغْلَظَ فَٱسْتَوَىٰ عَلَىٰ سُوقِهِۦ يُعْجِبُ ٱلزُّرَّاعَ لِيَغِيظَ بِهِمُ ٱلْكُفَّارَ وَعَدَ ٱللَّهُ ٱلَّذِينَ ءَامَنُوا۟ وَعَمِلُوا۟ ٱلصَّٰلِحَٰتِ مِنْهُم مَّغْفِرَةً وَأَجْرًا عَظِيمًا ٩ ﴾

"Muhammad is the Messenger of Allah. And those who are with him are severe against the disbelievers, and merciful among themselves. You see them bowing and falling prostrate (in prayer) seeking bounty from Allah and His Pleasure. The mark of them (i.e. the mark of their Faith) is on their faces (foreheads) from the traces of prostration. This is their description in the Torah. But their description in the Injil (i.e. the Gospel) is like a seed which sends forth its shoot, then makes it strong, and becomes thick and it stands straight on its stem, delighting those who sowed (it), that he may enrage the disbelievers with them." [Al-Fath: 29]

The Ruling Concerning the One Who Hates the Companions

Al-Imam Maalik ﷺ said, "Whoever has rage within his heart toward any companion of the Messenger of Allah ﷺ then this verse (i.e. Al-Fath: 29) applies to him." Allah ﷺ said,

> ﴿ وَٱلَّذِينَ ءَامَنُوا۟ وَهَاجَرُوا۟ وَجَٰهَدُوا۟ فِى سَبِيلِ ٱللَّهِ وَٱلَّذِينَ ءَاوَوا۟ وَّنَصَرُوٓا۟ أُو۟لَٰٓئِكَ هُمُ ٱلْمُؤْمِنُونَ حَقًّا لَّهُم مَّغْفِرَةٌ وَرِزْقٌ كَرِيمٌ ٧٤ ﴾

"And those who believed, and emigrated (i.e. the Muhaajiroon) and strove hard (i.e. made jihad) for the cause of Allah, as well as those who gave (them) asylum and aid (i.e. the Ansaar) - these are truly the believers, for them is forgiveness and a generous provision." [Al-Anfaal: 74]

The Variation in Degrees of Virtue amongst the Companions

Allah ﷺ differentiated between the companions who spent (for His Cause) and fought (in His way) prior to Al-Fath (i.e. the Victory, the Treaty of Al-Hudaybiyyah) and those who spent and fought afterwards. Although Allah has promised Heaven for both groups. He ﷺ said,

$$\{ \text{لَا يَسْتَوِي مِنكُم مَّنْ أَنفَقَ مِن قَبْلِ ٱلْفَتْحِ وَقَٰتَلَ أُوْلَٰٓئِكَ أَعْظَمُ دَرَجَةً مِّنَ ٱلَّذِينَ أَنفَقُوا۟ مِنۢ بَعْدُ وَقَٰتَلُوا۟ وَكُلًّا وَعَدَ ٱللَّهُ ٱلْحُسْنَىٰ وَٱللَّهُ بِمَا تَعْمَلُونَ خَبِيرٌ ۝} }$$

"...Not equal among you are those who spent before Al-Fath (i.e. the Conquest) and fought; those ones are higher in degree than the ones who spent after that and fought (after that). But to all Allah has promised the best. And Allah is All-Aware of what you do." [Al-Hadeed: 10]

The Prohibition of Insulting the Companions
It is collected in Bukhari and Muslim that Abu Sa'eed Al-Khudri reported that The Messenger of Allah ﷺ said, "Do not insult my companions. For indeed, if one of you were to spend (i.e. spend for the Cause of Allah) like the amount of the Mountain of Uhud in gold, you would not reach a mudd (i.e. an ancient Arabic measurement that is two hands of an average man cupped together) of what they spent or even half of that.'" A mudd is a quarter of a Saa', and half of that (which is mentioned in the hadith), means half of a mudd. This means that he (i.e. a person who comes after them and spends all that wealth) does not reach their (level of) virtue in that small amount (they spent), and not even half of that.

The Testimony of the Messenger of Allah that the Companions are Upon Goodness
Also, in Bukhari and Muslim on the authority of 'Imraan Bin Husayn ﷺ who reported that the Prophet ﷺ said, "The best of people are my generation then those who come after them, then those who come after them." 'Imraan (then) said, "I don't know if he mentioned after his generation two or three generations." ('Imraan continued narrating what the Prophet ﷺ then said), "Then there will be after them a people who give testimony, but they were not requested to give testimony and they will betray and they will not be relied upon (entrusted) and they will make vows but not fulfill them, and obesity will be apparent amongst them."

The Virtue of the Ansaar
It is also collected in Bukhari and Muslim on the authority of Anas ﷺ, that the Prophet ﷺ said, "The sign of faith is love for the Ansaar and the sign of hypocrisy is hatred for the Ansaar." And it is collected in Bukhari and Muslim on the authority of Al-Baraa' Bin 'Aazib ﷺ that the Prophet ﷺ said concerning the Ansaar, "No one loves them except a believer, and no one hates them except a hypocrite. Whoever loves them, then Allah loves him. And whoever hates them, then Allah hates him."

In Sahih Muslim it is narrated on the authority of Abu Hurairah from the hadith of Abu Sa'eed (may Allah be pleased with them both) that the Prophet ﷺ said, **"A man who believes in Allah and the Last Day will not hate the Ansaar."** It is collected in Bukhari and Muslim from the hadith of 'Ali Bin Abi Talib ؑ that the Prophet ﷺ said in the story about Hatib Bin Abi Balta'ah, **"...Indeed he had witnessed (the battle of) Badr. And what will make you know, that Allah might have looked upon the people of Badr and said, 'Do as you will, for indeed I have forgiven you.'"**

The Virtue of the Companions of the Pledge of Ar-Ridwaan

It is collected in Sahih Muslim on the authority of Jaabir Bin 'Abdullah ؑ who said, **"Umm Mubashshir informed me that she heard the Prophet ﷺ say in the company of Hafsah, 'No one will enter the fire, in shaa Allah, from the Companions of the Tree, those who gave the pledge underneath it.'"** They were 1400 in number. From amongst them was Abu Bakr, 'Umar, 'Uthman, and 'Ali.

The Ranking of the Companions with Regards to Their Virtue

Ahlus-Sunnah believe that the best of this Ummah, after its Prophet ﷺ, is Abu Bakr As-Siddeeq and then 'Umar Al- Faarooq. This is the consensus of the companions and the tabi'een (i.e. those who came after them and studied with them and followed them). None of them differed concerning this. Furthermore, it has been related in mutawaatir (i.e. an oft-recurring authentically reported hadith) form that 'Ali Bin Abi Talib said that **"The best of this Ummah, after its Prophet ﷺ, is Abu Bakr and then 'Umar."** Ahlus-Sunnah declare 'Uthman Bin 'Affan to be the third (best) and 'Ali Bin Abi Talib to be the fourth (best). May Allah be pleased with them both.

Section 12: The Correct Creed Concerning the People of the Household of the Messenger of Allah

From the beliefs of Ahlus-Sunnah wal Jamaa'ah is having love for Ahlul-Bayt (i.e. the people of the household) of the Messenger of Allah ﷺ, recognizing their virtue and honorable position. This is acting in accordance with the admonishment of the Prophet ﷺ the day of Ghadeer Khum, where he praised Allah, commended Him, admonished (the ummah), gave a reminder, and then said,

> To proceed: Indeed, oh people, indeed I am only a man and the Messenger of my Lord (i.e. the Angel of Death) is about to come to me and I will respond, and I will leave amongst you two heavy things, the first of them is the Book of Allah, in it is the Guidance and the Light, so take the Book of Allah and hold fast to it." So, he encouraged (the people) toward the Book of Allah and urged (them) to it. And then he said, "And the people of my household, I remind you of Allah concerning the people of my household, I remind you of Allah concerning the people of my household, I remind you of Allah concerning the people of my household.[47]

Ibn Kathir said in his Tafsir: "**And we do not reject those who admonish** concerning Ahlul-Bayt (i.e. the people of the Prophetic Household) nor the order to have Al-Ihsaan (i.e. good and kind treatment) towards them or to respect them and honor them, for indeed they are from a pure offspring from the most noble household ever found on the face of the Earth in terms of honor, esteem, lineage, specifically if they are followers of the authentic Sunnah which is clear and manifest, just like their forefathers were, like Al-'Abbaas and his children and 'Ali, the people of his household and his descendants ﷺ."

---

[47] Collected by Muslim, from the narration of Zayd Bin Arqam.

The Wives of the Prophet ﷺ are From His Household

They are from the people of his household ﷺ. Allah ﷻ said in a context where He is addressing them,

$$ \text{﴿ وَقَرْنَ فِى بُيُوتِكُنَّ وَلَا تَبَرَّجْنَ تَبَرُّجَ ٱلْجَٰهِلِيَّةِ ٱلْأُولَىٰ وَأَقِمْنَ ٱلصَّلَوٰةَ وَءَاتِينَ ٱلزَّكَوٰةَ وَأَطِعْنَ ٱللَّهَ وَرَسُولَهُۥٓ إِنَّمَا يُرِيدُ ٱللَّهُ لِيُذْهِبَ عَنكُمُ ٱلرِّجْسَ أَهْلَ ٱلْبَيْتِ وَيُطَهِّرَكُمْ تَطْهِيرًا ۝ وَٱذْكُرْنَ مَا يُتْلَىٰ فِى بُيُوتِكُنَّ مِنْ ءَايَٰتِ ٱللَّهِ وَٱلْحِكْمَةِ إِنَّ ٱللَّهَ كَانَ لَطِيفًا خَبِيرًا ۝ ﴾ } $$

"And stay in your houses and do not display yourselves like the displaying of the times of ignorance and perform As-Salat and give Az-Zakat and obey Allah and His Messenger. Indeed, Allah wishes only to remove Ar-Rijs (i.e. evil deeds and sins) from you, Oh Ahlal-Bayt (i.e. people of the Prophetic Household), and to purify you with thorough purification. And remember that which is recited in your houses of the verses of Allah and Al-Hikmah (i.e. the Wisdom, the Prophetic Way). Indeed, Allah is Ever Most Courteous, Well-Acquainted with all things." [Al-Ahzaab: 33-34]

Ibn Kathir said in his Tafsir (in explanation of the latter part of the first verse), **"And this is a text which shows that the wives of the Prophet ﷺ are included amongst Ahlul-Bayt (i.e. the People of the Prophetic Household), as they are the reason for the revelation of this verse...."**[48]

Also incorporated in this verse is the Leader of the Believers, 'Ali Bin Abi Talib, Faatimah the daughter of the Messenger of Allah ﷺ, Al-Hasan, and Al-Hussein (the two children of Faatimah and 'Ali), may Allah be pleased with all of them. This is based on the narration reported by 'Aaisha in Sahih Muslim (may Allah be pleased with her), **The Messenger of Allah ﷺ came out in the morning, wearing a type of garment made from black fur. Then Al-Hasan bin 'Ali came out. So, he brought him into the garment. Then Al-Hussein came, and he entered with him. Then Faatimah came, so he brought her in. Then 'Ali came so he brought him in** and then he quoted the verse:

$$ \text{﴿ إِنَّمَا يُرِيدُ ٱللَّهُ لِيُذْهِبَ عَنكُمُ ٱلرِّجْسَ أَهْلَ ٱلْبَيْتِ وَيُطَهِّرَكُمْ تَطْهِيرًا ۝ ﴾ } $$

"...Allah only intends to keep ˹the causes of˺ evil away from you and purify you completely, O members of the ˹Prophet's˺ family!" [Al-Ahzaab: 33]

---

[48] Quote abbreviated by Translator.

Section 13: The Correct Belief Concerning the Miracles of the Awliyaa

Ahlus-Sunnah wal Jamaa'ah believe in the existence of miracles from Allah for His Awliyaa (i.e. believing righteous servants) which were related in the prophetic narrations in an authentically recurring manner.

The Definition of a Wali

A wali) according to (the scholars of Islam) is someone who performs the obligatory actions according to the Islamic Law and stays away from that which the Islamic Law prohibited. Allah ﷻ said, concerning the Awliyaa,

﴿ أَلَآ إِنَّ أَوۡلِيَآءَ ٱللَّهِ لَا خَوۡفٌ عَلَيۡهِمۡ وَلَا هُمۡ يَحۡزَنُونَ ۝ ٱلَّذِينَ ءَامَنُواْ وَكَانُواْ يَتَّقُونَ ۝ ﴾

"Indeed, certainly the Awliyaa of Allah there is no fear upon them nor shall they grieve. They are˺ those who are faithful (i.e. they have Iman) and are mindful ˹of Him˺ (i.e. they have taqwaa)." [Yunus: 62-63]

Al-Walaayah (i.e. being close and beloved to Allah) is a product of true Iman and Taqwaa.

Definition of Al-Karaamah

A karaamah (i.e. a miracle) is a supernatural miraculous occurrence, which Allah makes happen at the hands of a wali from his Awliyaa, as an aid to him in an affair that can be related to religion or worldly life. However, the karaamah of a wali does not reach the level of the mu'jizaat (i.e. inimitable miracles) of the Prophets and Messengers (may the peace and commendations of Allah be upon them all.)

Some of the Miracles of Allah for His Awliyaa

From the miracles of Allah for His Awliyaa is the story of the companions (i.e. the youth) of Al-Kahf. Another example is the story of Mary (the mother of Jesus, peace be upon them both) when the pains of childbirth drove her to the trunk of a date-palm tree. So, Allah ordered her to shake the trunk of the date-palm tree towards her so that it would let fresh ripe dates fall upon her.

Allah provided for her by making the fruits of winter present with her in the summer and the fruits of summer present with her in the winter.[49] And also there is the story of Asif the scribe of Sulayman, the story of the man who Allah caused to die for 100 years and then resurrected him,[50] the story of Jurayj the Monk.[51] There is the story of the group of three from the Children of Israel who sought shelter in a cave and then a boulder closed them up in it.[52] And there are other examples which are well-known amongst the people of knowledge, affirmed in the Qur'an, the authentic Sunnah, or is authenticated about the predecessors and those who came after them.

Miracles are present in this Ummah until the establishment of the Day of Judgement. They are the result of Al-Walaayah (i.e. being beloved and close to Allah). And Al-Walaayah will continue until the establishment of the Hour. Whoever comes with some supernatural affair, this (alone) is not something that makes him praiseworthy or indicates his walaayah (i.e. his being beloved or close to Allah) until all his deeds are measured by the Qur'an and the Sunnah. So, only then it will be known whether this person was really a wali by his conforming to them and his following of (divine texts), both inwardly and outwardly.

The Virtues of a Wali

From the virtues of a wali is what Al-Bukhari narrated in his authentic collection on the authority of Abu Hurairah 🙏 who said, "The Messenger of Allah, 🕌 said, 'Indeed Allah proclaimed, 'whoever opposes a wali of mine, I have declared war upon him'.'"

---

[49] See the explanation of verse 37 of Surah aal 'Imran
[50] This story is mentioned in Surah al-Baqarah, Verse: 259
[51] Mentioned in Sahih al-Bukhari
[52] Mentioned in Sahih al-Bukhari

Section 14: The Correct Creed Concerning Obligations Towards the Muslim Rulers

Ahlus-Sunnah wal Jamaa'ah believe that Allah obligated upon the believers to obey those in authority over their affairs, except if it involves disobedience to Allah. They believe in the meaning of the Prophet's ﷺ statement in a narration reported on the authority of 'Ubaadah Bin As-Saamit رضي الله عنه:

> Listen and obey in your times of difficulty and in your times of ease and when you are motivated and when you are not motivated (i.e. because you dislike what you were ordered with) and when preference is made over you (i.e. they prefer themselves and their family and associates over you in wealth and positions) even if they oppressively take your wealth and strike your backs. (But don't obey) if you are ordered to do an act of disobedience.[53]

(Ahlus Sunnah) believes that it is prohibited to rebel against the people in authority even if they oppress and transgress as long as they do not see from them open and clear disbelief which they have a clear proof from Allah for. This is due to the statement of the Messenger of Allah ﷺ, **"The best of your rulers are those who you love, and they love you. You pray for them, and they pray for you. While the worst of your rulers are those who you hate, and they hate you. You curse them and they curse you."** It was said, **"Oh Messenger of Allah shouldn't we fight them with the sword?"** He responded, **"No, if they establish the Salat with you. And if you see from your rulers something that you hate, then hate his action. And do not remove a hand from obedience (i.e. don't rebel)."** And in another wording (of the same narration), **"...Whoever has a ruler placed over him and sees him do something that is disobedience to Allah, then he should hate what he has done from disobedience to Allah, and**

---

[53] Ibn Hibbaan cited this narration in his Sahih with a good chain of narration, and its origin is in Al-Bukhari and Muslim.

he (i.e. the person who saw the disobedience from his ruler) should certainly not remove a hand from obedience (i.e. he should not rebel)."[54]

The Consequences & Punishments for the One Who Rebels Against Rulers

The one who leaves the group (of Muslims united under their ruler), the Legislator (i.e. Allah) has set for him severe consequences in the worldly-life and in the Afterlife that suit the enormity of his crime. The one who dies while being in a state of rebellion (against the Muslim authorities) and separate from the group (of Muslims united under their ruler), has died a death of jaahiliyyah (i.e. the times of pre- Islamic ignorance). He is not even to be asked about, which is an indication of the gravity of his sin. Whoever splits from the group (of Muslims united under their ruler) has no excuse with Allah on the Day of Judgment, and the devil is with him infiltrating and striving to make mischief. A whoever splits from the Muslims, his blood becomes permissible.

Ahlus-Sunnah wal Jamaa'ah Believe in Praying for the Rulers

Ahlus-Sunnah wal Jamaa'ah believe that praying for the ruler is praiseworthy and certainly good (according to the Sunnah). This is a sign of a man being from amongst Ahlus-Sunnah, as Al-Imam Al-Barbahaari said in *Kitaab As-Sunnah*: **"If you see a man praying against the Sultan, then know he is a person of desires. And if you hear a man praying for the Sultan to be upright, then know he is a person of the Sunnah, in shaa Allah (i.e. Allah willing)."**

Al-Fudayl Ibn 'Iyyaad[55] said, **"If I had one supplication (that was sure to be answered) I would not make it except for the Sultan. Because we were ordered to pray for them to be upright and we were not ordered to pray against them even if they oppress and transgress, because their oppression is upon themselves and upon the Muslims. While, their being upright is for themselves and for the Muslims."**

Al-Imam As-Saabunee said in *The Creed of the Predecessors, Companions of the Hadith*, **"And they have the view that they (i.e. the Muslim rulers) should have prayer made for them that they be reformers and that they be granted success and be upright. And they see insulting them (i.e. the Muslim rulers) as something that has been prohibited in the legislation due to the agreement of the major companions of the Messenger of Allah 拳."**

---

[54] This narration was cited by Muslim on the authority of 'Awf Bin Maalik.
[55] **Translators Note**: Al-Fudayl bin 'Iyyaad was from the scholars of the early generations of Muslims. He died in the year 187 after the hijrah.

Anas Bin Maalik said, **"Our leaders, from the companions of the Messenger of Allah 🌸, prohibited us - he said - Do not insult your leaders, do not cheat them, do not hate them, fear Allah, and have patience. For indeed the affair is near (i.e. the Day of Judgment is near)."**[56]

---

[56] Abu 'Aasim narrated this in his As-Sunnah and others.

Section 15: The Prohibition of Disputing Concerning the Religion

Ahlus-Sunnah wal Jamaa'ah forbid argumentation and disputing in religion matters, as the Prophet ﷺ prohibited. In the al-Bukhari and Muslim it is related that the Prophet ﷺ said, **"Recite the Qur'an as long as your hearts are in harmony, but if you differ with each other (over it) then stop it (i.e. stop reciting or reading)."**[57] It is reported in the Musnad and the Sunan of Ibn Majah – its origin is in Sahih Muslim – on the authority of 'Abdullah Bin 'Amr Bin Al-'Aas, **that the Prophet ﷺ came out whilst people were disputing concerning the Qadar (i.e. Predestination). It was if a pomegranate seed was split open in his face (i.e. his face was very red) due to his anger." So, he said, "Is this what you were ordered to do!? Or is this what you were created for!? You strike some of the Qur'an against other parts of it!? Through this the nations before you were destroyed."**

Rather, a narration has been reported indicating that disputing and argumentation is a chastisement from the punishments of Allah upon this Ummah. In the Sunan At-Tirmidhi and Ibn Majah it is reported from the narration of Abu Umamah who said, The Messenger of Allah ﷺ said, **'No people became misguided after having guidance, except that they were given al-jadl (i.e. arguing, disputation).'** Then he recited,

$$﴿مَا ضَرَبُوهُ لَكَ إِلَّا جَدَلًا ۚ بَلْ هُمْ قَوْمٌ خَصِمُونَ ٥٨﴾$$

"...They did not cite this example for you except for argument. In fact, they are a people prone to dispute...." [Az-Zukhruf: 58)

---

[57] **Translator's Note:** In the explanation of this narration by Sheikh Ibn Al-Uthaymin, he mentioned that this means that if you are in a gathering and you are reading or reciting the Qur'an or if you are going over any issues of knowledge and benefitting from it and your hearts are in harmony then do it. But if you begin to differ to the point where your differing will cause intense argumentation and dispute that may even lead to fighting then cease your reading in this situation to avoid trouble.

Al-Imam Ahmad ﷺ said, "The Foundations of the Sunnah are: Holding firmly to the way of the Companions of the Messenger of Allah ﷺ and taking them as an example. (It is to) leave off innovations, for indeed every innovation is misguidance. (Also, it includes) leaving off debating and argumentation, not sitting with the people of desires; it is to abandon debating and argumentation in the religion."

Blameworthy Debating

(This prohibition) is concerning argumentation with falsehood, disputing about the truth after it has been made clear, arguing about an issue which the one who is debating has no knowledge about, arguing about those concepts in the Qur'an which are elusive, or arguing whilst having the wrong intention, etc.

The Praiseworthy Debating

Debating is praiseworthy, when done by a person of sound knowledge, correct intention, and is debating to clarify the truth, while adhering to proper decorum. Allah ﷺ said,

﴿ ٱدْعُ إِلَىٰ سَبِيلِ رَبِّكَ بِٱلْحِكْمَةِ وَٱلْمَوْعِظَةِ ٱلْحَسَنَةِ وَجَٰدِلْهُم بِٱلَّتِي هِيَ أَحْسَنُ ﴾

"Invite to the Path of your Lord with wisdom and fair preaching and argue with them in a way that is better." [An-Nahl: 125]

He ﷺ said,

﴿ * وَلَا تُجَٰدِلُوٓاْ أَهْلَ ٱلْكِتَٰبِ إِلَّا بِٱلَّتِي هِيَ أَحْسَنُ ﴾

"And do not argue with the People of the Scripture (i.e. the Jews and the Christians) unless it is in a way that is better..." [Al-'Ankabut: 46]

And He ﷺ said,

﴿ قَالُواْ يَٰنُوحُ قَدْ جَٰدَلْتَنَا فَأَكْثَرْتَ جِدَٰلَنَا فَأْتِنَا بِمَا تَعِدُنَآ إِن كُنتَ مِنَ ٱلصَّٰدِقِينَ ٣٢ ﴾

"They said, 'Oh Noah! You have disputed with us and much have you prolonged the dispute with us, now bring upon us that which you threaten us with, if you are from the truthful ones." [Hud: 32]

Some Islamically Legislated Debates

Allah ﷺ informed about Abraham's ﷺ debating with his people and Moses's ﷺ debating with Pharaoh. Likewise in the Sunnah, the debate between Adam and Moses is mentioned, may peace and commendations be upon them both.

The righteous predecessors were reported to have had many debates. All of them were examples of the praiseworthy type of debating, in which the following conditions are present:

- Knowledge
- The Correct Intention
- Following (the Prophetic Way)
- The Manners of Debate

Section 16: A Warning against Associating with the People of Desires

Ahlus-Sunnah wal Jamaa'ah strictly warn against sitting with the people of desires and innovations. For it is in opposition to Allah's command and a sign of harboring love for them. The one who sits with them is in danger of complying with their misguidance and following them upon their falsehood.

Ibn Taymiyyah (may Allah have mercy on him) said, **"The innovation by which a man is considered to be from the 'people of desires' is that which is well known by scholars of the prophetic way– to contradict the Qur'an and Sunnah such as the innovation of the Khawaarij (i.e. the Rebels, Renegades who rebel against the Muslim authorities deeming it to be part of the religion), the Rawaafid (i.e. the Rejectionists, a sect of Shi'ites), the Qadariyyah (i.e. those who deny the pre-decree of Allah), and the Murji'ah (i.e. those who do not deem actions to be a part of faith)."** Allah ﷻ said:

﴿ وَإِذَا رَأَيْتَ ٱلَّذِينَ يَخُوضُونَ فِىٓ ءَايَٰتِنَا فَأَعْرِضْ عَنْهُمْ حَتَّىٰ يَخُوضُوا۟ فِى حَدِيثٍ غَيْرِهِۦ ۚ وَإِمَّا يُنسِيَنَّكَ ٱلشَّيْطَٰنُ فَلَا تَقْعُدْ بَعْدَ ٱلذِّكْرَىٰ مَعَ ٱلْقَوْمِ ٱلظَّٰلِمِينَ ۝ ﴾

"And when you (Oh Muhammad) see those who engage in a false conversation about Our Verses by mocking at them, stay away from them until they turn to another topic. And if Satan causes you to forget, then after the remembrance do not sit in the company of those who are the wrong-doers." [Al-'An'aam: 68]

Abdullah bin 'Abbas ﷜ said, **"Until the Day of Judgement, every person who introduces something new into the religion and every innovator is included in this verse."** Al-Baghawee reported this statement in his Tafsir, attributing it to Ibn 'Abbas. Ibn Jareer At-Tabari ﷺ said, **"There is an explicit indication in this verse about the prohibition of sitting with every kind of people of falsehood when they engage in their misguidance, whether they be innovators or wicked sinners."** Ibn 'Abbaas ﷜ said, 'Do not sit with the people of desires. For indeed sitting with them sickens the hearts.'[58]

---

[58] Collected by Al-Aajurri in *Ash-Shariah* (1/453)

All praise is due to Allah. It is only by His granting of guidance and success, that the book, *The Correct Creed Which Every Muslim Must Believe*, is complete. I ask Allah to make this deed sincerely for His Noble Face and in accordance with the Sunnah of His Prophet Muhammad ﷺ. (I ask) that He allows the masses of Muslims to benefit from it.

May the peace and commendations of Allah be upon our Prophet Muhammad, the pure people of his household, his righteous companions, and whoever follows them with Ihsaan until the Day of Judgement.